FRENCH-ENGLISH CONTRASTIVE LEXICOLOGY

SÉRIE PÉDAGOGIQUE

DE L'INSTITUT DE LINGUISTIQUE DE LOUVAIN — 14

J. VAN ROEY

French-English Contrastive Lexicology

An Introduction

PEETERS

LOUVAIN-LA-NEUVE

1990

D. 1990/0602/83 ISBN 90-6831-269-3

Printed in Belgium

CONTENTS

PART TWO : FRENCH-ENGLISH CONTRASTIVE LEXICOLOGY

What's in a name? That which we call a rose
By any other name would smell as sweet.

W.Shakespeare
Romeo and Juliet, II.ll.43

PREFACE

This book is based on a number of lectures given to students of English at the Université Catholique de Louvain. My purpose in those lectures was to provide students with an introduction into lexical semantics and to give them some insight into the diverging and converging ways in which the data of human experience are reflected in the lexical material of French and English.

Part One of this volume therefore confronts the student briefly with some of the problems which have always been topical in lexical semantics: How can its basic unit, the word, be defined? What is meant when we say that a word «has meaning»? How does the semantic content of a word develop? How do relations between form and meaning content lead to the distinction between homonymy and polysemy? What types of meaning relations do words enter into? What are the specific procedures linguistics has proposed to analyze word meaning, and to what extent are they applicable and do they reveal general structural aspects of the lexicon?

Part Two represents the actual contrastive approach. Apart from a brief discussion of the theoretical issues raised by contrastive lexicology, it basically aims at showing in what sense and to what extent semantic equivalence between French and English vocabulary items is limited and virtually as rare as intralinguistic synonymy. The conceptual, connotative, stylistic and collocational differences which account for such partial or deceptive equivalence are successively surveyed. The final chapter of this second part is devoted to the pitfalls represented by the presence in the two vocabularies of such large numbers of items which are formally similar but semantically different, i.e.to faux amis.

Two appendices, respectively presenting some critical spelling differences and a selective list of dictionaries, complete this introductory survey.

My claim to originality or innovation, not only in the baffling area of semantics but also in the analysis of the French and English vocabularies, is quite modest. The selective bibliography at the end of the book is of course meant to help the interested student, but at the same time to indicate that I owe very much to very many.

Special thanks are due to Mrs. Helen Swallow, who kindly accepted to read the manuscript and suggested important corrections and valuable improvements.

PART ONE

BASIC CONCEPTS

INTRODUCTION

I.LEXICON.LEXICOLOGY

The term *lexicon* has been used in different senses in linguistics. In its most common sense it is used as a synonym of «vocabulary» and refers to the total stock of the words of a language. If this definition is adopted (as we shall do in this survey), the seven items which appear between blank spaces in the sentence *The gardener's wife seems to be recovering* all belong to the lexicon of the English language.

In another, more restrictive, sense the term *lexicon* is used by some linguists to cover only «content» words, i.e. words which have «lexical meaning» (such as *gardener*, *wife*, *seem* and *recover* in the example given), to the exclusion of «function words», i.e.words with «grammatical meaning» (such as *the*, *to* and the progressive marker *be*. See I.2).

Other scholars, on the contrary, use the term in a wider sense, viz.to refer to all the basic structural elements of the morphological system of the language, i.e.not only words, but also parts of words which have no independent existence (= bound morphemes). In the illustrative sentence above, the elements *-er*, *-s*, *-s*, *re-* and *-ing* are, according to this view, as much part of the lexicon as the seven items *the*, *gardener*, *wife*, *seem*, *to*, *be*, and *recover*.

It is to be noted, finally, that transformational-generative grammarians use the term in yet a different sense. To them the lexicon is, along with phonology and syntax, one of the components of the complete description of the language system. This lexical component contains not only all the words of the language, but also all the information about their structural characteristics, i.e.their semantic, syntactic and phonological properties.

As mentioned already, *lexicon* will in this survey be used in its most common, general sense of «vocabulary». However, as our contrastive approach focuses on lexical meaning, we shall be concerned almost exclusively with «content words».

Of course, defining the lexicon as the «total stock of the words of a language» raises the further problem of what exactly is meant by «words». This is the subject of the following paragraph.

Lexicology is the scientific study of the lexicon. As words have both a form and a meaning, the lexicologist may be concerned with problems of form (the structure and formation of words) or with problems of meaning (the meanings of words and the meaning relations between words). The terms «lexical morphology» and «lexical semantics» are often used to distinguish these two aspects of lexicology.

When problems of word meaning are discussed, a distinction may be made between *semasiology* and *onomasiology*. In a semasiological approach, the investigator starts from the form of a lexical unit and studies the meaning(s) it expresses. He will say, for instance, that the English word *kid* means 1° young goat, and 2° child. In an onomasiological approach, he starts from a given meaning or concept and studies the lexical items which express it. Thus he will find that the meaning «non-adult human being» is rendered in English by the items *child*, *kid*, *brat*, etc.

The study of the form as well as the study of the meaning of words may be undertaken from a synchronic or from a diachronic point of view. *Etymology* is the name of the discipline concerned with the historical evolution of lexical items. Before the appearance of structuralism most of the work done on the vocabulary of languages was of an etymological nature.

A discipline related to, but different from, lexicology is *lexicography*. This term denotes the art and science of dictionary making, and is thus in a sense applied lexicology.

The history of linguistics shows that the phonological and grammatical structure of language has received much more attention than the lexicon.There is both a quantitative and a qualitative reason for this. First of all, whereas the phonological and grammatical units of a language are limited in number and form a closed system, vocabulary items form an open, unlimited set: words fall into disuse and disappear, but others are constantly being created or borrowed from other languages and added to the existing stock (e.g.F.*gaulliste*, *mère porteuse*, *fioul*, E.*ayatollah*, *moped*, *smog*), so that the lexicologist's object of study is a huge and fluctuating mass of data. Secondly, from a qualitative point of view, the phonologist and the grammarian mainly deal with problems of form; the lexicologist, on the other hand, mainly tackles problems of meaning content, i.e. problems which have psychological and philosophical aspects, where scientific rigour is much harder to achieve, and where the answers given are often necessarily vague. Thus, whereas linguists have relatively clear insights into the systems formed by the phonemes and the grammatical constituents of language, their understanding of the meaning relations between the lexical units of language is much more limited. This clearly emerges from the fact that the main source of information about the vocabulary of a language is still the dictionary, which is merely a list of separate items, classified in alphabetical order, a principle which in no way reflects the network of semantic relations between these items. Only dictionaries of synonyms and antonyms present two aspects of this network in a relevant way.

Yet it is clear that vocabulary is all-important, for we can communicate in a foreign language if we know words, but not if we know only sounds and grammatical rules. Sounds and grammatical patterns are meaningless in themselves, and only serve to form and combine the words of the language. The vocabulary is «language's window onto the world of non-linguistic experience, the level on which language reaches out, so to speak, from its system of symbolic forms and patterns to the non-linguistic entities that these forms and patterns are designed to represent: a word always «refers», in some way, to something outside itself» (Dagut 1977, 223).

II.WORD, LEXEME

As stated above, the units which make up the vocabulary of a language are usually called «words». This common term is part of every man's basic vocabulary and seems to represent an entity whose existence and nature raise no problems. Don't we say that «speaking» means «using words», and don't we notice that all language learning starts with the acquisition of words? Yet considerable problems do arise when the linguist attempts to define the term «word» scientifically. In fact it defies exact definition, as does the term «sentence», and as do some other basic linguistic terms.

To define the word in terms of spelling habits as the linguistic form occurring between two blank spaces is only acceptable to non-specialists. First of all because some little-known languages are mainly used for oral communication and hardly ever written, and secondly because spelling habits, even in world languages like English, may be to some extent arbitrary and unsystematic. There are no scientific grounds, for instance, for considering *wintertime* and *mudguard* as one word, and *winter sports* and *mud bath* as two words. Similarly, one fails to see why F.*pomme de terre* should be treated differently from *carrotte* with regard to word status.

A well-known definition is the one proposed by the American linguist L.Bloomfield, according to which the word is « a minimal free form ». This would certainly apply to items such as *milk*, *home*, *good*, *to run* etc., or F.*chat*, *bleu*, *dire*, etc. which are all « minimum forms » in the sense that they cannot further be subdivided, and « free » in the sense that they can be used by themselves (for instance in answers to questions : « What would you like to drink ? » -« Milk »). However, Bloomfield's definition would not be applicable to such items as *wintertime*, *mudguard* or *pomme de terre*, which contain more than one « free form », or to *the* or *and*, which are not free.

According to a more recent and more satisfactory definition proposed by John Lyons (1968, 202), words are linguistic units characterized by internal stability and uninterruptability. Both these criteria indeed distinguish words from phrases or clauses. Whereas the order of elements which make up a clause can often be rearranged (*all the men came : the men all came*, F.*grave erreur*, *erreur grave*), no such rearrangement is possible in compound forms such as E.*wintertime*, *mudguard*, *winter sports*, *mud bath*, *each other*, *in spite of*, F.*pomme de terre*, *casse-noix*, *parce que*, or in derived forms such as E.*worker*, *undo*, *friendly*, F.*rapporteur*, *déformer*, *rapidement*, which are all internally stable and therefore words. As to the second criterion, whereas the sequence making up a phrase or a clause can usually be interrupted (E.*all the pupils* : *all the new pupils*, *the students protested* : *the students immediately protested*, F.*tous les élèves* : *tous les nouveaux élèves*, *les étudiants ont protesté* : *les étudiants ont immédiatement protesté*), the sequence making up a word cannot. In fact these criteria point to a basic characteristic of the forms which linguists classify as words : their high degree of cohesion.

It will be noticed that these criteria allow the lexicologist also to treat as words the fixed combinations or sequences of words which are usually called « idioms » (e.g.*red tape*, *to kick the bucket*, F.*bas bleu*, *casser sa pipe*), for they too are internally stable and uninterruptable. Besides, they show a high degree of cohesion from a semantic point of view in that they express one global meaning, which cannot be derived from the meanings of the individual elements they contain.

Yet, helpful though they are, Lyons' criteria have no absolute value. Most linguists, for instance, tend to see English phrasal verbs (*give up*, *turn off*, *let down*) as single words because of their cohesive nature, even if they are interruptable combinations (*give it up*, *turn them off*, *let us down*). This simply means that there is no clear-cut division between words and word combinations, which is not surprising in view of the fact that cohesion is a relative quality. In this survey we shall use the term « word », with « lexical unit » or « lexical item » as synonyms, whenever the degree of cohesion seems to justify this, but without trying to adopt absolutely valid criteria.

But there is a second problem with words. If we identify *sing* as a word, will we say that *sings*, *sang*, *sung* and *singing* are different words? Are F.*viens*, *viennent* and *venez* three different words? Linguists have suggested the term «lexeme» to cope with this difficulty. Just like the phoneme and the morpheme at other levels of linguistic analysis, the lexeme is an abstract entity representing different concrete realizations in actual language, i.e.all the different forms one and the same «word» may take. Thus English has an abstract entity or «lexeme» SING, which in actual usage may appear as *sing*, *sings*, *sang*, *sung*, *singing*, as it has a lexeme MAN, which manifests itself in actual language use as *man*, *man's*, *men* or *men's*, and as French has a lexeme VENIR with a large number of different realizations (*viens*, *viennent*, *venez*, *venons*, *venu*, etc.).

CHAPTER I: LEXICAL MEANING

I.1.WORD = FORM + MEANING

The words of language have a form, which we can physically perceive in speech and in writing, and a meaning, which teachers and linguists explain by using other words.

Form and meaning are inseparably united in the word. A sound or a sound combination to which no meaning corresponds (say, « English » *turp* or « French » *cilpe*) cannot be called a word, and neither can a meaning which is not expressed by a given sound or combination of sounds.

It is a characteristic of all communication systems that the relation between the form and the meaning of their signs or symbols is conventional: there is an agreement between those who use them to use well-defined forms to express well-defined meanings. This holds true, for example, for the Morse code and for traffic signs, and also for human language. Yet there is a difference between these systems. The Morse code is not only conventional, it is also purely arbitrary: the groups of dots and dashes (and the corresponding sounds) which represent letters and numbers have been chosen once and for all in a completely arbitrary way. The system of traffic signs on the other hand, while also conventional of course, is motivated: there is a natural link between, for instance, the picture of a child crossing the street and the message, which is something like « drivers, be careful, for children regularly cross the street in this area ». Human language, to some extent, comes in between. For the very large majority of words the relation between form and meaning is purely arbitrary: there is no reason or necessity to call a tree « tree », except that there is a convention in the English speech community to call it so. Other speech communities have decided to call a tree « arbre » or « Baum », etc., and communicate just as efficiently. However, beside this vast majority of « unmotivated » or « opaque » word forms, all languages have a number of « motivated » or « transparent » ones. Basically, this motivation may be of three different types:

1° Phonetic motivation. This is first of all the case with onomatopeia, i.e.words such as E.*cuckoo*, *cock-a-doodle-doo*, *bang*, *crack*, *hiss*, *moo*, *splash*, *zoom*, etc. or F.*gazouillis*, *roucoulement*, *boum*, *crac*, *vrombir*, etc., whose phonetic structures directly imitate the sounds they denote. Next there is also a relation, though of a more mysterious kind, between phonetic form and meaning in so-called phonaesthetic words, i.e.in words where a given sound or sound combination produces a given sensory or emotive effect. Thus English words with initial *gl-* often suggest an idea of light or shining (*glimmer*, *glint*, *glisten*, *glitter*, *gleam*, *glow*); words in *-ump* are often associated with heaviness and dullness (*hump*, *lump*, *thump*, *stump*); English and French items with *i* frequently denote smallness (E.*bit*, *tip*, *pip*, *sip*, F.*petit*, *joli*, *mignon*, etc.), while such as have initial *fl-* often suggest a smooth and airy movement (E.*fly*, *flee*, *flutter*, *flow*, F.*flot*, *flotter*, *fluide*, *flute*, etc.). But in all these cases the motivation is only relative. This is clear from the fact that onomatopeia may be markedly different from one language to another (compare E.*cock-a-doodle-doo* and F.*cocorico*, E.*moo* and F.*beugler*, and that it is quite easy to think of «exceptions» to the sound symbolism just described: *glum* = sad, in low spirits; *to flag* = to be or become weak and less active or alive; *big* evokes precisely the opposite of smallness.

2° Morphological motivation. Compounds like E.*housekeeper*, *toothbrush*, *home-made*, *to underpay*, F.*couvre-lit*, *garde-chasse*, *sous-développé*, *survoler*, and derivations such as E.*co-pilot*, *replay*, *worker*, *timeless*, *beautify*, F.*défaire*, *préjuger*, *travailleur* or *fortifier* will easily be understood even by speakers of English or French hearing them for the first time, as their morphological structure makes them transparent (at least if the speaker or learner is familiar with the simple constituents which they contain). This is not always the case, however, as some compounds and derivations have meanings which cannot be derived from the constituent elements and are therefore «opaque». E.*blue-stocking*, *ladybird* and *howler*, or F.*bas-bleu*, *franc-maçon*, and *quatre-de-chiffre* are only a few examples.

3° Semantic motivation. Words are semantically motivated when there is transfer of meaning from the basic sense to a derived, figurative sense. Examples of this highly productive and creative device are legion in most languages: E. *the eye (of a needle)*, *the neck (of a bottle)* , *to drown (one's sorrows)*, F.*le pied (d'une montagne)*, *le mur (du son)*, *(un commerce) florissant*, etc. etc. In the course of time such motivation may disappear, as is the case for most contemporary speakers of English and French with, for example, *breakfast* or *crane* and *déjeuner* or *grue*. But this does not make the meanings of these «unmotivated» words less clear, which shows that motivation is not essential to the communication process.

I.2. LEXICAL MEANING vs. GRAMMATICAL MEANING

In the first paragraph of our Introduction a distinction was made between two basically distinct types of words: function words (or grammatical words) and content words (sometimes also referred to as lexical words). Let us take, as a new example, the sentence *The songs and poems have been recorded* and go a little more deeply into this distinction.

If one analyses the words of this sentence from the point of view of what they contribute to its understanding, one notices that some of them only represent the structural devices or categories the English language makes use of. Thus *the* represents «definiteness», *and* «coordination», whereas *have* and *be* respectively stand for the «perfectivity» and «passiveness» of an activity or event, which are all grammatical categories of English (and of many other languages). *The*, *and*, *have* and *been* may therefore be termed «function words» or «grammatical words», as they only convey grammatical meaning. The items *songs*, *poems* and *record*, on the other hand, are «content words»: they have meanings which have nothing to do with the mechanism of the linguistic system itself; they are clearly related to some parts or aspects of the world around us, i.e.they have non-grammatical or lexical meaning.

The difference between the two kinds of meaning, it is true, is less clear-cut than it might seem at first sight. The grammatical system and the lexical system interact in an intricate way in language. First of all some grammatical categories have a non-grammatical connection: thus «perfectiveness» has something to do with «past time». Secondly, all lexical words always have some grammatical meaning as well. Thus we call *song*, *poem*, *boy*, *house* etc. «nouns» because they all share certain grammatical properties in English: for instance, they all occur in typical functions (subject, object) in sentences. Nevertheless, the difference between the two kinds of meaning is real, and is parallelled by a formal opposition: function words form closed classes (i.e. articles, conjunctions, auxiliaries etc. are limited in number and new ones cannot be added to the vocabulary), whereas content words constitute open classes (i.e.there are large numbers of nouns, verbs, adjectives and adverbs, and new ones are regularly added to the stock). In addition, the relative frequency of function words is much higher than that of content words: on any page of a book or newspaper items like *the*, *this*, *of* or *and* are sure to occur many times, whereas such common nouns as *man* or *house* may not occur at all.

I.3. LEXICAL MEANING

I.3.1. PRELIMINARIES

The study of meaning («semantics») is an extremely arduous and complex undertaking. First of all because meaning in language can be studied at different levels: the meaning of a text (its «message»), the meaning of a sentence (which depends not only on the words which occur in it, but also on grammatical factors such as word order, for example), the meaning of a word (which is our particular concern) or even of a morpheme (*pre-* vs *post-*, for instance), and because specific problems arise at each of these levels. Secondly and more importantly, because meaning has to do with mental processes, with relations between linguistic forms and the extra-linguistic world, with relations between these linguistic forms, so that semantics is of interest not only to linguists, but also to philosophers, psychologists and sociologists. This also makes it difficult to gain an overview of the field, for the many different approaches to the problem of meaning have resulted in a very confusing terminology, whereby such basic terms as «meaning», «sense», «denotation» or «reference» are often used in different ways by different schools of scholars.

It is not surprising, therefore, that many fundamental questions of meaning are still unanswered and hotly debated, even if great progress has been achieved since Bréal coined the term «sémantique» around 1900. «Pity the poor analyst», Bolinger says in «Aspects of Language» (1975, 205), «who has to do the best he can with meanings that are as elusive as a piece of wet soap in a bathtub». It is clear that, within the limits of this survey, we can only hope to give some essential elements.

A second preliminary, more particularly with regard to word meaning, has to do with an objection that is sometimes made, viz. that words have no meaning in themselves, but that their meaning is determined each time they are used by the context in which they occur, by the intention of the speaker or writer, and by the particular speech or writing situation.

It is of course true that the meaning of words is context-dependent. In *Why did they kill the elephant?* and in *I had some time to kill* the verb *kill* will have two different interpretations, and the same is even true of *go* in *It takes twenty minutes to go from Marble Arch to Picadilly Circus* (where *go = walk*) and in *It takes about twenty minutes to go from Dover to Canterbury* (where *go = drive*). It is also true that the meaning of words is user-dependent: house painters and housewives have different things in mind when they use the word *brush*, for instance. Finally, meaning is also situation-dependent, for example in the sense that the word *ceremony* does not cover the same reality in a church as in a university.

The answer to the objection is simply that the lexicologist or the lexicographer must be aware of the different senses in which words are used according to context, user and situation, and must account for these different uses in as far as they are part of the language system, i.e.in as far as they are systematic and thus based on social convention. To take the examples just given: in his analysis of *kill*, the dictionary writer will thus distinguish the sense «cause to die» from the sense «spend» (and from other senses in which the verb may be used); in the case of *go*, *brush* and *ceremony* he will find that the different modes of going, the different kinds of brushes, and the different types of ceremonies cannot all be viewed as different meanings of these words, as might be said in the case of *kill*. He will observe that the words *go*, *brush* and *ceremony* are conventionally used in a general way, covering slightly different realities, and he will, in conformity with this usage, capture these in a basic «definition» in his dictionary.

Admittedly, a speaker or writer may be creative and innovative in his use of the language. A poet may use the word *journey* to refer to «life», or a person in love may refer to his beloved by using the word *canary*, for instance, and the meanings of these items would indeed be incomprehensible if removed from the context or situation in which they are used. They are incomprehensible because the use made of these words is not in accordance with the conventions of the English speaking community. The use of *journey* and *canary* in the senses just mentioned is not part of the language system, but an individual, isolated phenomenon, and therefore of no relevance to the lexicologist or the lexicographer.

After all, if nothing sensible or relevant could be said about the meanings of words without the presence of actual context or situation, dictionaries would be useless books, which is certainly contradicted by experience.

I.3.2. A DEFINITION TO START FROM

An attractive definition of lexical meaning is the following: the meaning of a word is the contribution this word makes to the correct understanding and interpretation of the sentence in which it occurs. This definition is attractive but obviously too vague, for it naturally raises the question: What is it and how is it that words contribute to the understanding and interpretation of sentences?

It seems justified to distinguish at least four points of view from which words make such contributions or, to put it differently, to distinguish at least four types of lexical meaning: a conceptual meaning (also «cognitive meaning»), a connotative meaning, a stylistic meaning, and a collocational meaning. We shall discuss these successively in the following sections.

I.4. CONCEPTUAL MEANING

The conceptual or cognitive meaning of a word is that aspect of lexical meaning which has to do with the language user's knowledge and experience of the extra-linguistic world, of reality. To define this vague description more precisely has been a matter of controversy for generations of linguists, philosophers and psychologists. The following paragraphs will present a short survey of the problems involved.

I.4.1. THE REFERENT THEORY

What is true of any symbol or sign also applies to the words of language: they represent something other than themselves. When we use words in actual communication we often refer through them to one or more particular persons, animals or things (whereby «things» is to be taken in its widest sense and includes not only physical objects, but also actions, activities, events, feelings, etc.etc.). This is the case, for instance, when I say *My cat is sleeping on the sofa*, where *cat* refers to the specific animal I keep in the house. The particular person(s), animal(s) or thing(s) thus referred to by words in actual utterances are the «thing(s) meant» or «referents» of these words.

The theory that the meaning of a word is its referent, put forward by some early semanticists and still lingering on in popular thinking, is no longer taken seriously nowadays. If indeed the meaning of a word were its referent, then

1° the word *cat* would have as many meanings as there are cats which people refer to;

2° the word *cat* would have no meaning at all in the sentence *Minnie is a cat*, where only *Minnie* has a referent, and where *cat*, used in predicative function, has no referent at all, but only denotes a property of the referent *Minnie*;

3° the items *morning star* and *evening star* would have identical meanings, as they are both used in English to refer to one and the same referent, viz.the planet Venus (Frege 1892).

Also, for many words of the vocabulary (*nothing*, *something*, *unimaginable* etc.etc.) it is difficult to see what part or aspect of the extra-linguistic world could be identified as their referents, and yet nobody would like to claim that they are meaningless.

It is nevertheless true that «meaning» can be equated with «referent» in the language of small children and in the use of proper nouns. When a two-year-old child uses the word *mother*, for instance, it uses this word as a name or label for one single referent, and adults use proper nouns such as *London*, *Einstein*, etc.in the same way. But this is marginal linguistic usage, and it is more justified to say that in these cases the words only have reference and lack meaning, rather than to claim that the meaning of these items is their referent.

It is worth noting that we have simplified things a little here, and that some semanticists (e.g.Lyons 1977) make a distinction between reference and denotation. According to this view, proper nouns are practically the only ones that have reference, i.e.are practically the only ones that refer to a particular person, animal or object in the real world, as in *Einstein won the Nobel prize for physics in 1921*, *Minnie has caught a mouse* or *Brussels is the capital of Europe*. Other words, for instance common nouns such as *cat* or *house*, can only be made to refer to particular objects when they are used in context, for instance when they are combined with a determiner (*the, my, this*), as in *My cat is sleeping on the sofa* or *This house is my grandfather's*. When not used in such contexts, these words have no reference, but only denotation, i.e.they denote classes of people, animals or things or, put differently, they relate in a general way to people, animals or things in the real world. However, this distinction does not solve our problem of word meaning: if it was difficult to see what the referent could be of *something*, *nothing*, *unimaginable*, etc., it is equally difficult to see what their denotation might be.

I.4.2. The image theory

According to a theory that has a long tradition, the meaning of a word is a «mental image», i.e.an image which is present in the brain of the speaker and hearer each time the word is used in communication. The reasons why this theory is unacceptable are obvious. First of all, if it is true that we can «visualize» the content of such vocabulary items as *horse*, *book*, *fish* or *cigarette*, there are also very many others where this seems doubtful or impossible. *Thought*, *situation*, *nihilistic*, *possible* or *true* are only a few examples. Secondly, mental images are entities located in the psyche of the individual and may therefore be different from one occasion to the other and from one individual to the other, so that they cannot be used as a sound basis for scientific study. What is the mental image representing the meaning of *work*, for instance? Is it that of a miner slaving away in a shaft, or that of a farmer ploughing his field, or that of an office worker bent over his word processor? It can be all these images and many more. Finally, the conceptual content of many words cannot be reduced to visual properties: thus the difference between *smoke* and *steam* has more to do with how they are caused than with physical appearance, and the difference between *to murder* and *to assassinate*, which may evoke the same image, is a matter of intent (*to assassinate* = to murder for political reasons).

I.4.3. THE CONCEPT THEORY

This theory, which also goes back to the early days of linguistic theory but still lives on in the work of more recent linguists, is in fact a weakened version of the image view of meaning. It sees the meaning of a word as a mental, though not necessarily visual entity, a «capsule of thought» as the American linguist Sapir put it, which is associated in our minds with the word form. Thus the word form *house* corresponds to a «concept» or «capsule of thought» or, more simply, a «thought» or «idea» HOUSE, which embraces, not just one or more given individual houses (referents), but our whole experience of houses.

Ferdinand de Saussure («Cours de linguistique générale», 1916) and Ogden & Richards («The Meaning of Meaning», 1923) are among the exponents of this theory. The former defines the word as «une unité psychique à deux faces, (qui) unit non une chose à un nom, mais un concept (or «signifié») à une image acoustique (or «signifiant»)» (98-99). Similarly, Ogden & Richards point out that there is no direct relation between word form and referent or «thing»; the word form only refers to the «thing» via the concept.

The objections raised with regard to the concept theory are basically the same as those that lead linguists to reject the image view of meaning. What traditional linguists call «concept» is something vague and elusive, something strictly individual and therefore only observable by the unreliable method of introspection but not accessible to scientific analysis. After all, to say that the meaning of a word is a concept is simply to replace one vague term by another, so that nothing is gained.

There is, of course, no doubt that, when we use words or hear them used, there are mental processes at work which associate these words with our experience of the extra-linguistic reality. How this conceptualization takes place is a psychological problem the linguist cannot solve; what takes place in the minds of a speaker and hearer when they communicate is not accessible to him. The only thing he can do is observe the communication process in an objective way and try to put forward a hypothesis that explains its hidden mechanisms. With regard to semantics (including word meaning) the distinctive feature theory (or «componential analysis») is such a hypothesis.

I.4.4. THE DISTINCTIVE FEATURE THEORY. COMPONENTIAL ANALYSIS

The distinctive feature theory (or «componential analysis») sees the conceptual meaning of a word as a complex or bundle of semantic features or components which are linguistically relevant in the sense that they condition the correct use of the word and distinguish it from the use of other words in the language.

When we say that a person knows the meaning of a word, we mean that he uses the word correctly, i.e.according to the conventions or «rules» of the language. Thus a speaker of English knows the meaning of the word *bull* if he uses it to refer to the well-known bovine adult male animal. If, on the other hand, a speaker (e.g.a child during the learning process) uses the word *bull* to refer to a cow or a calf, or to a horse or a pig, we will say that he does not know its meaning. It is thus clear that conceptual meaning has to do with our knowledge and experience of the world, so that meaning rules may be expressed in terms of conceptual features referring to characteristics of «things meant». However, of all the characteristics «things meant» may have in reality, only some are «linguistic», i.e.have linguistic relevance. Bulls, for instance, are heavy, four-legged animals, more than three feet in height and more than six feet in length, equipped with a relatively long tail, and with a white, red or black coat; they are kept on farms, are mainly used for breeding, ruminate and make a bellowing sound; they are males of the bovine family, whose females are cows and whose young are calves. People with specialist knowledge, vets for instance, will further tell us that bulls belong to the Theria class of animals, that they have two-hoofed legs, etc. Not all these features are relevant to the linguistic meaning of the word *bull*. The only ones that are linguistically relevant are those that constitute the necessary and sufficient conditions for the correct use of the word *bull* in English, i.e. those that serve to distinguish its use from the use of any other word in the language. These distinctive features are only three in number: /bovine/, /adult/ and /male/[1]). They are indeed necessary, for the feature /bovine/ is needed to distinguish *bull* from *stallion* for instance, whereas the feature /adult/ distinguishes it from *calf*, and /male/ distinguishes it from *cow*. They are also sufficient: the

---

1 A full description of all the characteristics of bulls therefore does not have its place in dictionaries (which deal with language), but in encyclopaedias (which deal with things). It is true that many dictionaries often also give encyclopaedic information, either for practical reasons (to please their readers) or for theoretical ones (i.e. the

features «used for breeding» or «with long tail», for example, are not distinctive, in the sense that there is no other word in the English vocabulary whose meaning is different from that of *bull* only because it lacks the component « used for breeding» or «with long tail».

Componential analysis of meaning, mainly represented by the American linguists Katz and Fodor (1963, 1966), has much in common with the analytical methods used in modern phonology, whereby phonemes are represented as bundles of distinctive features of sound (bilabial, nasal, voiced, etc.). It is often used successfully to show meaning relations between semantically related words more systematically and economically, usually in the form of a matrix and using plus or minus signs:

	/bovine/	/adult/	/male/
bull	+	+	+
cow	+	+	-
calf	+	-	±

It is easy to take a further step in the study of the English vocabulary on the basis of this analysis, and to relate this group of items to the group *man*, *woman*, *child*, which is distinct from it on the basis of one feature (/human/ instead of /bovine/), or to the group *stallion*, *mare*, *foal* on the basis of /horse/ instead of /bovine/.

As another illustration of such componential analysis, consider Pottier's well-known treatment of French «siège»-words (1963), for which he sets up six features («sèmes» in his terminology): /pour s'asseoir/, /sur pied/, /pour une personne/, /avec dossier/, /avec bras/, /avec matériau rigide/. The lexeme *siège* itself has only the first feature, which, however, it shares with all the other items, and for which reason it is called the «archilexème» (superordinate term). *Pouf*, *tabouret*, *chaise*, *fauteuil*, *canapé* differ from each other in that they all have or combine different features:

	S1	S2	S3	S4	S5	S6
chaise	+	+	+	+	-	+
fauteuil	+	+	+	+	+	+
tabouret	+	+	+	-	-	+
canapé	+	+	-	+	+	+
pouf	+	-	+	-	-	-

---

difficulty there may be,as we shall see, in identifying the distinctive semantic features of an item).

Of course, the components which distinguish related meanings are not always physically observable, as they are in the two examples just given. They may be of an abstract or complex nature, and therefore much more difficult to detect and formulate. In his treatment of the verbs of judging in English, Fillmore (1968) shows, for example, that *to accuse*, *to credit*, *to criticize* and *to praise* are to be semantically differentiated on the basis of 1° what is presupposed, and 2° what is claimed:

	PRESUPPOSITION			CLAIM		
	act is bad	act is good	B is respon-sible	act is bad	act is good	B is respon-sible
A *accuses* B of...	+					+
A *credits* B with...		+				+
A *criticizes* B for...			+	+		
A *praises* B for...			+		+	

I.4.5. Componential analysis: Weaknesses

However attractive componential analysis may seem at first sight because of its more economical and more systematic nature, it is far from solving the problems of lexical semantics. Most of the criticisms levelled at it tend to show that it cannot adequately cope with the vagueness for which the traditional concept theory was rejected.

First of all there is some vagueness with regard to the actual status of the components. If the meaning of *man* is analysed as a set of three semantic features, /human/, /adult/ and /male/, one may wonder what the real nature of these components is. They cannot, of course, be the meanings of the English WORDS *human*, *adult* and *male*, for the whole idea of componential analysis is to break down concepts into minimal units (« atoms ») of meaning, which cannot be words (for then they would in turn be made up of minimal units). Advocates of componential analysis claim that components are not part of the vocabulary of the language itself, but basic cognitive elements (« primitives ») in terms of which the human mind conceptualizes. This implies that they are universal, i.e. that they underlie the structure of all languages. If this is perhaps acceptable for some basic features such as /animate/, /human/ or /male/, it certainly is not for the subtle distinctions used in many componential descriptions (as in Lehrer's description of containers, where /sealed lid/ and /replaceable lid/ are among the components used to distinguish *can* from *jar* in English). Thus the notion of component lacks clarity of status, and its universal validity is not convincing.

Secondly, some of the features used in componential analysis are inherently relative and therefore vague. This may be the case, for example, when components are represented by adjectives. When these are in binary opposition (such as /alive/: /dead/, /male/: /female/), things are simple and clear: the negation of one feature unambiguously implies confirmation of the other, so that /-alive/ or /-male/ automatically mean /+dead/ or /+female/. However, in the case of «polar opposites» such as /old/: /young/ or /large/: /small/ this is not so, for these pairs are in fact extreme points on a scale where in-betweens exist. Thus /-old/ and /-large/ do not necessarily mean /+young/ and /+small/, but can be interpreted as /+middle-aged/ and /+middle-sized/. Also, the quality expressed by such features is relative to a norm, which raises an additional problem, difficult to cope with in componential analysis: *large* in the sentence *My house is large* means «large for a house», which is in fact small in comparison with, for instance, a large city.

Finally, words like *man* and *woman*, *bull* and *cow* refer to «things» which belong to clearly structured categories in reality, and it is therefore relatively easy to express their meanings in terms of distinctive features: /+human/, /+adult/, /+male/ and /+human/, /+adult/, /-male/ clearly and completely distinguish the meanings of *man* and *woman*, and so do the sets of components /+bovine/, /+adult/, /+male/ and /+bovine/, /+adult/, /-male/ with regard to the meanings of *bull* and *cow*. But many other vocabulary items refer to «things» which have features that are not neatly distinguishable, so that their meanings have «fuzzy edges», i.e. contrast only vaguely and cannot be adequately described in terms of components. Consider verbs referring to noises, for instance (E.*scream*, *screech*, *squeak*, *squeal*, *yell*, etc.), or to light (*gleam*, *glisten*, *glitter*, *glow*, etc.). For lack of a metalanguage the componential analyst cannot do any better than the traditional semanticist. The same holds true for the semantic distinction between e.g. words which refer to natural classes, such as *fruit* and *vegetable*, *tree* and *bush*, *mountain* and *hill*. If we represent *fruit* as /+growing on a tree or bush/, /+containing seed/, /+used for food/, then this certainly applies to *apple*, *pear*, *cherry* etc., but what about *tomato*, which is generally seen as a vegetable? Many linguists nowadays share the view that «relatively few lexemes are plausible candidates for componential analysis» (Lyons 1981, 154).

It may be noted in passing that, in order to cope with problems raised by such «class words» as *fruit* etc., some semanticists have developed a «prototype» approach to componential analysis (Rosch et al.1975, Lakoff 1982). In this approach, words are seen as having a central or nuclear sense, a prototypical kernel, with blurred edges and fuzzy boundaries, so that a distinction is made between central members or prototypes of a given category (i.e.those which possess the largest number of features of the category, e.g.*apple*, *pear*, *cherry* etc. of the category *fruit*), and more peripheral members, more or less loosely linked to the prototypical sense (e.g.*tomato*, *cucumber* etc.).

Other linguists, inspired by recent work in philosophy and logic (e.g.Tarski's theory of truth), have abandoned any approach whereby words are put in direct correspondence with what they denote in the real world. They prefer to see word meaning in terms of the systematic contribution a word makes to the truth conditions of sentences in which it occurs.

I.4.6. CONCEPTUAL MEANING CONCLUDED

As one linguist put it, from the point of view of the psychology of the speakers of a language, words are «labels for experiences» (Hanks, 1979). Thus a native speaker of English knows what the words *truth* or *knowledge* or *bull* or *fruit* mean because he has heard these items used and has used them himself on countless different occasions and in countless different contexts, so that they are an integral part of his experience as a social human being. But the linguist faces the hard task of discovering those features of experience which are necessary and sufficient to explain linguistic behaviour and to predict it. That there is as yet no fully adequate or generally acceptable method to do this should not come as a surprise if one considers that the vocabulary of a language consists of a huge number of «signs» (words) which form a very heterogeneous group in that they perform very different semiotic functions in the communication system. Apart from grammatical words, some items refer to concrete «things» of all sorts, others to abstract «things»; of the latter, some will express actions, states, events, processes or qualities, others circumstances in which actions etc. take place, attitudes towards them, logical or temporal relations between them, etc. As already mentioned, in some cases the relations between such words seem relatively clear and their meanings can be described fairly accurately; in many other cases the relations between these items form extremely complex networks and contrasting dimensions may be very vague.

To some extent componential analysis has provided the vague notion of «concept» with a more objective and concrete content, and represents a more economical and systematic approach to the problem of word meaning. However, it has considerable shortcomings, and is therefore of limited applicability.

I.4.7. THE THEORY OF USE

The many difficulties inherent in the analysis of conceptual meaning have led some linguists to adopt an «operational» approach to the problem of word meaning. This approach is based on the view that « the meaning of a word is its use in the language » (Wittgenstein 1953, 20) or, put differently, that « the meaning of a word is to be found by observing what a man does with it, not what he says about it » (Chase 1938, 7). Thus the meaning of the lexical item *cow* could, according to this theory, best be explained by simply showing all the contexts and situations in which this item occurs in the English language. To know the meaning of *cow* simply means knowing how the word is used correctly in English.

As we have seen, it is of course true that correct use of the language is conditioned by knowledge of the meanings of its words, and, conversely, that the way a word is used by the speakers of a language determines its meaning, but this does not imply that the use of a word IS its meaning. As Ullmann puts it, « the use of a word, its distribution, the collocations in which it enters, are not identical with its meaning; they are consequences and manifestations of the meaning, even if, for methodological reasons, one may feel that it is through these consequences that meaning can be most profitably be explored » (1971). If the meanings of words were to be defined in terms of their occurrence with other words, this would necessarily lead to a circular process : if *cow* is « defined » on the basis of, say, *moo* and *milk* (*cows moo*, *cows give milk*), the words *moo* and *milk* will in turn have to be defined on the basis of their occurrence with *cow*.

For practical purposes a combination of the analytical approach and the operational approach may turn out to be useful. After all, lexicographers tend to apply both in order to describe the meanings of words : they will first describe them analytically (usually in the form of a definition), and then illustrate their uses in typical contexts.

I.4.8. Sense

From what has been said so far it will be clear that the meaning of many words may be seen as having two distinct aspects : one that is determined by its relation to the extra-linguistic world, and one that is determined by the relation of the word to other words in the vocabulary. The first meaning aspect may be illustrated by the description we gave of the meaning of bull in one of the previous chapters : « an adult male bovine ». For the second meaning aspect the term « sense » is often reserved; we refer to the sense of bull when we say, for instance, that its meaning is included in that of animal, that its meaning is connected with those of *cow* and *calf* in the same way as the meaning of *stallion* is connected with those of *mare* and *foal*, that of *father* with those of *mother* and *child*. Hyponymy, synonymy, antonymy etc. are therefore sense relations.

In fact there are, then, two kinds of semantics: one that deals with meaning in the light of our experience of the world, and one that deals with meaning as relations between words, though the two are of course interdependent. Whereas theoretical semanticists will naturally focus on « sense », the intra-linguistic aspect of meaning, which leads to insight into the structure of the lexicon, lexicographers cannot afford to disregard the inter-linguistic aspect, as their ultimate aim is to supply their readers with referential or denotational information. In this survey the two terms will not be systematically distinguished.

I.4.9. A NOTE ON DICTIONARY DEFINITIONS

The difficulty in defining the meanings of words is reflected in the way dictionaries cope with this problem, and it may therefore be useful to devote a short digression to it.

Lexicographers use several methods to make the meaning and use of words clear to their readers. The most current ones (Robinson 1962, Benson, Benson & Ilson 1986) are:

1° The analytical method, which is the classical method of defining, going back to Aristotle. It consists in determining first the general class to which the « thing » defined belongs, and then the characteristics which distinguish it from the other members of the class. Or, to put it in more technical terms, to determine first the « genus » and then the « differentiae ». The definition of *cow* by the Longman Dictionary of Contemporary English, « the fully-grown female form of cattle, kept on farms, especially to give milk » is an example: « cattle » is to be seen as the genus, and « fully-grown », « female », « kept on farms » and « giving milk » as the differentiae.

If we compare this analytical description of *cow* with the features proposed in our componential analysis of the same item in I.4.4., we notice that they partially overlap. As was pointed out, the purely linguistic meaning is determined by those features which are necessary and sufficient, but, as dictionaries are not written for linguists, they tend to be more encyclopaedic. It is true, however, that the componential analysis of the conceptual meaning of a vocabulary item is in some cases nothing but a formalized representation of the traditional definition.

2° The synthetic method, which relates the « thing » denoted by a word to other « things ». It brings « things » together, i.e. synthesizes them. Thus, when *circle* is defined as « the figure drawn by a line moving in a plane with one end fixed » (Waldron 1967, 55), the « thing » is in fact defined by relating it to its cause. Similarly, when *red* is defined as « the colour of blood or of the ruby », it is defined by relating it to where it can be found. It is true that synthetic definitions are often also partially analytical: in the definitions just given, «figure» and «colour» are analytical elements.

A special variety of the synthetic definition is the so-called «formulaic» definition, often used in the case of adjectives, whereby the «formulas» *of, from* or *relating to* are typically used: *Canadian*: *of or relating to Canada or its people*; *linguistic*: *of, relating to language*; *medieval*: *of the Middle Ages.*

3° The synonym method: This method in fact does not define at all; it simply tells the dictionary user that a given word has the same meaning as another word, e.g.*tibia*: *shinbone*. However, the equivalence of synonyms is usually limited to their conceptual content; from the point of view of style or register (as in *tibia* vs. *shinbone* or in *policeman* vs. *cop*) or from the point of view of connotation (as in *slim* vs. *skinny*) they may be far from equivalent.

4° The implicative method, also called citation method. Here again, nothing is explicitly defined. The meaning of a word is shown by the way it is used in a suitable context. Example: *disguise*: *he went to the ball in the disguise of a clown..*

5° The denotative method. This merely consists in citing examples of the «things» denoted by the lexical item, as when *cereal* is «defined» as: *wheat, rye, barley, rice, etc.*

6° The ostensive method, which is used when the referent of the word is represented by a picture or a photograph.

7° The rule-giving method, which is used with grammatical or function words (*but, as, who, him*), and simply consists in indicating a rule for their use. Thus *him* may be «defined» by means of the comment «the form of *he* used as direct or indirect object of the verb».

I.4.10. CONCEPTUAL MEANINGS ARE LANGUAGE-SPECIFIC

It is commonly believed that the world of reality around us, with all the distinctions and classifications we make in it, is independently given, is independent of language. It is assumed that the world of experience is a very complex but objectively structured set of «things» (people, animals, plants, objects, events, properties, etc. with all the categories we distinguish in them), on each of which each language «sticks its own label», i.e.for each of which each language has its own specific word.

It is of course true that many of the distinctions made in the real world are common to many languages. Thus most languages, if not all, will distinguish *man* from *woman* in their vocabularies, *father* from *mother*, *night* from *day*, *dead* from *alive* or *big* from *small*, and the more closely related languages are, the more striking the correspondences will be. But anyone familiar with translation work knows only too well that even in such cases one-to-one correspondence of conceptual meaning is limited: translating is rarely a simple operation whereby words of language A are simply replaced by words «with the same meaning» in language B; quite often it is complicated by the fact that language B «has no word» (or no fully equivalent word) for a particular meaning expressed by a given item in language A.

Man's experience of reality can in fact be seen as a continuum of sense impressions, thoughts and emotions, which each language cuts up and categorizes, partially according to objective data, but partially also according to the consciousness of the linguistic community. Or, if one prefers, man's experience of the extra-linguistic world can be viewed as a vast multitude of features which each language crystallizes into units (words) in the way it finds appropriate. Words therefore do not passively reflect a pre-existent organisation of the world around us; they themselves partially impose this organisation upon us. As Martinet puts it, «en fait, à chaque langue correspond une organisation particulière des données de l'expérience. Apprendre une nouvelle langue, ce n'est pas mettre de nouvelles étiquettes sur des objets connus, mais s'habituer à analyser autrement ce qui fait l'objet de communications linguistiques» (1960, 16). A classical example of this language-specificness of conceptualisation or «découpage différent de la réalité» is that of the colour spectrum. Though the physical reality of this natural continuum is the same for speakers of all languages, different vocabularies may cut it up in different ways (See Berlin & Kay, 1969). Whereas English operates with eleven basic colour terms (*black*, *white*, *red*, *green*, *yellow*, *blue*, *brown*, *purple*, *pink*, *orange* and *grey*), Russian has twelve (with two types of blue), Tamil, a language spoken in India, has five, and Ibo, a Nigerian language, only four.

This is how the activities of eating and drinking are categorized in the vocabularies of four different languages (Corneille 1976, 105):

IRANIAN	FRENCH	GERMAN	TAMANACO (Brazil)
		essen (human)	*jucuri* (eat bread)
	manger		*jemeri* (eat fruit)
		fressen (animal)	*janeri* (eat meat)
khordan			
		trinken (human)	
	boire		
		saufen (animal)	

In the area of beef-cattle both English and French make use of the feature /sex/ to distinguish *cow*, *vache* from *bull*, *taureau*, and of the feature /adult/ to distinguish *calf*, *veau* from the other two. Some African languages, however, also have specific words to distinguish white cows from black or red ones, for instance.

As mentioned above, different lexicalisation of concepts is of course less marked in languages which are culturally and historically more closely related, but it is nevertheless real. *Assassinate* and *assassiner* are a case in point: English selects a feature /political/ to distinguish *assassinate* from *murder*, whereas this feature is irrelevant in French: *assassiner* is /+ or - political/. In the same way English distinguishes *wounded* from *injured* according to whether war or fighting is or is not involved, while French has only *blessé*. Conversely, French makes use of a feature /flowing to the sea/ and on this basis differentiates *fleuve* from *rivière*, whereas English overlooks this distinction and has only *river*.

It is worth noting in passing that language-specificness is not limited to the lexicon, but is observable on the level of grammar as well. Where Chinese makes no distinction for gender, French has a twofold system (*il*, *elle*) and English a threefold one (*he*, *she*, *it*). Where French and English distinguish singular from plural, Arabic and Basque make a threefold distinction for number (singular, dual, plural in the former case; singular, plural, undetermined in the latter). And further examples are numerous.

This language-specificness of conceptual meaning, this lack of isomorphism between languages finds its theoretical explanation in the very nature of language: language is form given to substance. This applies first of all to the «plane of expression» (which is not our main concern here), in the sense that each language gives its own «form» to the extra-linguistic reality of vocal sounds in that it selects its own phonemes and combines them in its own way. The same thing holds true on the «plane of content»: each language gives its own «form» to the extra-linguistic substance of human experience in that it selects its own conceptual features which account for specific meanings of words (Hjelmslev 1943, Catford 1965).

	LANGUAGE		
	FORM	FORM	
Phonic substance			«Situation» substance
	PHONOLOGY	LEXICON	
plane of expression		plane of content	

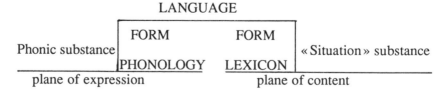

The fact that meanings are language-specific has led to the theory of linguistic determinism or linguistic relativity, going back to the ideas of the philosopher Wilhelm von Humboldt (1767-1835), and mainly represented by the American anthropologists and linguists E.Sapir and B.L.Whorf. According to this theory, the concepts a human being has, the way he views the world around him and interprets it are entirely imposed on him by the language he speaks. «We cut nature up», Whorf claims, «organise it into concepts, and ascribe significances as we do, largely because we are parties to an agreement that holds throughout our speech community and is codified in the patterns of our language. The agreement is, of course, an implicit and unstated one, but its terms are absolutely obligatory; we cannot talk except by subscribing to the organisation and classification of data which the agreement decrees» (in J.B.Carroll 1956, 213).

Two observations ought to be made here. First of all, that this theory is unacceptable in its extreme form. Secondly, that it gives only a partial, unilateral view of the relationship between language and culture.

Whereas all linguists would subscribe to the first part of Whorf's statement (i.e. to the language-specificness of meanings we have been dealing with in this paragraph), few would still be prepared to agree with the second part. For if our thinking, our view of the world of experience around us were ENTIRELY determined by the language we speak, speakers of different languages would be (to use Corder's image) like prisoners in different «mental straitjackets» and would be totally unable to learn another language or to translate from one language into another. This clearly is not the case. The fact, for instance, that we do not have a French or English translation equivalent for each of the three words denoting «to eat» in Tamanaco does not prevent us from grasping the concepts they represent and from expressing them, e.g. by means of a paraphrase (*eat bread*, *eat fruit*, *eat meat*). Inversely, speakers of Tamanaco and many other distant languages have perfectly mastered our Western tongues, even if their vocabularies and grammars reflect a different perception of reality on innumerable points. The theory of linguistic determinism is therefore only acceptable in its weak form, in the sense that different linguistic categorisation TO SOME EXTENT influences our thinking and our perception of reality, that it «predisposes us to certain choices of interpretation», as Lyons puts it.

A second observation is that, if the language of a speech community to some extent determines its view of reality, its culture, the reverse also holds true. Thus, if the vocabulary of the Eskimo language has at least five words for *snow* (corresponding to falling snow, wind-driven snow, snow on the ground, snow packed hard like ice, melting snow), whereas French and English have only one word, then this is of course to be ascribed to the fact that this natural phenomenon plays an all-important part in the culture of the Eskimo society. «The lexical distinctions drawn by each language will tend to reflect the culturally important features or objects, institutions and activities in the society in which it operates» (Lyons 1968, 432). Language thus influences our perception of reality, but the reality or culture in which we live also influences our language.

I.5. CONNOTATIVE MEANING

It is often the case that lexical items have the same conceptual meaning or «denotation», and yet are not absolute synonyms because of a different connotation. In addition to their conceptual or denotative meaning (i.e. the set of distinctive and therefore essential semantic features), words may indeed have a connotative meaning, i.e. secondary features, either of a conceptual or emotive or evaluative nature, which form a kind of «halo associatif» around the word.The most common opposition (but by no means the only one) expressed by connotation is that of «pejorative» vs. «ameliorative» (or «derogatory» vs. «appreciative»).

Connotation may have its origin in several factors. First of all it may be due to the specific form of words. When dealing with phonetic motivation, we have already pointed out the emotive or expressive value of some sounds or sound sequences in English and French vocabulary items (I.1). Thus the vowel *i* was said to evoke smallness in English (*bit*, *tip*, *pip*, etc.), and this appears to be the case in French as well: «pour la grande majorité des sujets, le i est perçu comme petit, clair et gentil», says Kerbrat-Orrechioni (1977, 30). Thus also, because of their initial consonant sequence *cr-*, E.*crack* and F.*craquer*are more expressive than their «synonyms» *break* and *se briser*. In poetic language more than anywhere else the suggestive or emotive value of words is readily exploited, for, as the popular singer Yves Duteil puts it, «la saveur des choses est déjà dans les mots» («La langue de chez nous»). In other cases it is the formal resemblance with another lexical item that accounts for the specific connotation of a given word. Thus F.*sansonnet* evokes «chanson», and is therefore a more suggestive name for the bird usually referred to as *étourneau*. In the English speaking world the followers of Sun Myung Moon do not appreciate being called «moonies», probably because of the association with *to moon about* (=to wander about or to behave in an aimless, unhappy way) and with *moonstruck* (=suffering from a slight form of madness). (Bolinger 1980, 20).

Not only the phonetic form, but also the morphological form of words may produce connotative effects. Thus English compounds (including phrasal verbs) and derivations often convey their conceptual meaning more suggestively and dynamically than their synonyms or than their French equivalents. Compare E.*four-legged* and E.*quadruped*, F.*quadrupède*, E.*to stand down* and E.*to resign*, F.*démissionner*, E.*to upgrade* and E.*to promote*, F.*promouvoir*.

Secondly, a given connotation may have to do with characteristics of the referent, the « thing meant ». Because most mothers are caring and affectionate, F.*mère* and E.*mother* have this particular connotation. Similarly, because E.*home* usually indicates the place where one likes to be and feels good, this item connotes warmth and safety. Because the integration of immigrants into our Western societies has caused some social problems, the words F.*immigré* and E.*immigrant* have an unfavourable connotation for some. Because of the social taboo on things to do with sex or some physiological functions, words such as E.*whore*, *fuck*, *arse* or F.*putain*, *baiser*, *cul* have a taboo connotation.

A third source of connotative meaning is the derived or secondary sense in which a word is used. This may be observed with the English items *peasant*, *intercourse* and *gay*, for instance, and with their French equivalents *paysan*, *rapport* and *gai*: because of the secondary sense of these items (respectively « unmannered person », « sexual intercourse », « homosexual »), the words *farmer* and *agriculteur*, *relation* and *relation*, *cheerful* and *joyeux* may be preferred by speakers of English and French.

It may be noted here that, when a vocabulary item has an unpleasant denotation or connotation, the language user may choose to resort to a « synonym » which lacks this particular flavour, i.e. a euphemism. A few examples are:

F	*vieux*	*âgé, d'un certain âge*
	aveugle	*handicapé de la vue*
	(crâne) chauve	*(crâne) dégarni*
	les morts	*les disparus*
	mourir	*décéder*
	ivrogne	*alcoolique*
	putain, prostituée	*fille*
	baiser, copuler	*faire l'amour*
	cul, derrière	*fesses*
	cul-de-sac	*voie sans issue*
	politicien	*homme politique*
	tromper, mentir	*induire en erreur*

	(pays) sous-développé	*(pays) en voie de développement*
E	*an old person*	*a senior citizen, an elderly person*
	deaf	*hard of hearing*
	the dead	*the departed*
	to die	*to depart, to pass away*
	drunkard	*alcoholic*
	whore	*prostitute*
	to fuck, to copulate	*to make love*
	arse	*behind, bottom*
	guerilla	*freedom fighter*
	to lie	*to mislead*
	underdeveloped (country)	*developing (country)*

In many languages, but especially in English, the euphemism may take the form of a foreign, especially a Latin word: *genitalia*, *excreta*, *faeces*, *libido*, etc. In such cases the unpleasant connotation is replaced by a learned or even a pedantic one.

As we have said, connotative features are not an essential part of a word's meaning. A person is a mother when the features /parent/ and /female/ can be applied, whether or not she is caring and affectionate; a referent is a home when the feature /dwelling place/ applies, whether or not it is warm and safe. Just because connotation is of a secondary order, it may vary from one individual to another, from one community to another, and from one period to another, according to different experiences of reality. Thus the word *dog* will have different connotations for a dog lover and for someone who was once bitten by a dog; the word *communist* does not have the same overtones in the USA and in the USSR; the word *atomic* was not much more than a technical term before the atom bomb killed over 75,000 people in Hiroshima in 1945; since the democratisation of our Western societies the words *élite* and *aristocracy* have taken on an unfavourable ring.

A good illustration of what connotation is all about may be given by quoting what some writers and journalists have had to say recently about the vocabulary problem connected with the increasingly frequent phenomenon of the unmarried couple:

« De nos jours, l'union libre se répand... On ne parlera plus de concubinage, mais de cohabitation juvénile ou de couple sans alliance. Cependant, les incertitudes du vocabulaire demeurent et reflètent bien les incertitudes des situations...D'ailleurs, les *cohabitants* ont beaucoup de difficulté de parler l'un de l'autre. Visiblement, bien qu'on utilise ces expressions, ni *mon copain/ma copine*, ni *mon ami(e)*, ni *mon compagnon/ma compagne* ne conviennent vraiment. Restent alors différentes circonlocutions, comme *celui/ celle avec qui je vis*, etc. La complication grandit encore quand il faut se situer par rapport au réseau de relations de chacun des partenaires, par rapport aux deux familles, sans parler du milieu de travail ou de l'administration...»

(Couple et mariage, R.Rezsohazy
La Libre Belgique, janvier 1984)

«L'administration reconnaît et utilise les mots *concubin, concubine, concubinage*. Moi, je les déteste. Je leur trouve un arrière-goût péjoratif et moralisateur qui s'explique d'ailleurs étymologiquement. «*Concubine*, du latin *concubina*: qui couche avec», précise le Robert...Je suggère, au choix, deux mots de remplacement: *compagnon* ou *cohabitant*. Ce dernier n'existe pas encore dans le dictionnaire, raison de plus pour l'officialiser. A moeurs nouvelles, mots nouveaux.»

(Entre vous et moi, C.Collange
Elle, 11 décembre 1978)

«The question of the unmarried couple is everywhere. How to handle the linguistic problem of what to call the person with whom one's daughter lives? *Lover* is too archaically lubricous by a shade or two. *Roommate* sounds like a freshman dorm. *Bedmate* is too sexually specific, but *friend* is too sweetly platonic. *Boyfriend* and *girlfriend* are a bit adolescent. *Partner* sounds as if they run a hardware store together. The Census Bureau calls them «Partners of the Opposite Sex Sharing Living Quarters» or *POSSLQS*.

(America's New Manners
Time Magazine, November 27th 1978)

Tournier (1985, 288) has collected the following amusing list of English words to denote such a person: *co-habitant*, *co-habitee*, *companion*, *co-vivant*, *domestic associate*, *live-together*, *meaningful associate*, *POSSLQS*, *significant other*, *special friend*, *ummer*, *URAM* (unrelated adult man), *URAW* (unrelated adult woman). «L'origine de *ummer*», he notes, « est cocasse: le père d'une jeune fille qui vit avec un jeune homme présente ce dernier à des amis avec embarras et dit: «This is my daughter's ...um...er...»»

It is not always easy to decide whether a given (ameliorative or pejorative) feature is or is not an essential part of the meaning of a word, so that it may be difficult to keep denotation and connotation apart. On the other hand it should be noted that there is some correlation between connotative meaning and stylistic meaning (see I.6 below), in the sense that vocabulary items belonging to certain types of style almost invariably produce certain types of connotation.

Connotation is of course not limited to language. It plays a part in other types of communication, e.g.in visual arts and more especially in advertising. Certain kinds of drinks or cigarettes, for instance, are advertised with images of sunny beaches and cheerful young people in order to associate the product with physical and moral health and to produce a favourable connotation.

I. 6. STYLISTIC MEANING

Two or more words may have the same conceptual meaning and yet differ from each other with regard to the situation or context in which they are used. Thus, while *mother* and *Mum* share the conceptual features /parent/ and /female/, the former item can be used in all situations, whereas the latter is limited to informal, even familiar usage. The two words will therefore be said to differ in stylistic meaning, which we define as the meaning of a word in so far as it is determined by the situation or the circumstances in which it is used.

As is well known, each language is in fact a system of sublanguages or varieties (with specific phonological, grammatical and lexical characteristics), which may be distinguished on the basis of a number of situational factors. We do not address our superiors in the same way as we talk to our friends;we do not use the same language in a scientific article as in a personal letter. Thus what we call «the English language» or «la langue française» has no real existence as such, but is in fact represented by a large number of closely connected varieties. For a language learner to keep these varieties apart, to use the right word in the right situation is often quite a problem.

The main factors which determine language varieties are:

- The social status of the user. From this point of view, a traditional distinction is that between «Upper Class English» and «Middle or Lower Class English», or «U» and «non-U» usage, although class distinctions are now less marked than they used to be. In the French-speaking world too, the preference for some vocabulary items and the avoidance of some others may be a matter of social prestige on the part of the user. A few examples are:

	NON-U	U
E.	*tea*	*supper, dinner*
	afters	*dessert*
	lounge	*sitting room, drawing room*
	to sweat	*to perspire*

toilet	*lavatory*
note-paper	*writing-paper*

F.	*patate*	*pomme-de-terre*
	maître	*instituteur*
	docteur	*médecin*
	soupe	*potage*
	suer	*transpirer*

- The relationship between users. As such relationships may range from very formal (e. g. between heads of state or diplomats) to extremely familiar (e. g. between brothers and sisters, boys in a football team), the linguistic forms used will range just as widely. To delimit varieties within that range and to label them is necessarily a delicate and to some extent subjective undertaking. The American linguist Martin Joos (1962) distinguished five language levels or « styles » : frozen, formal, consultative, casual, and intimate, which may be represented for instance by *join the heavenly choir*, *pass away*, *die*, *kick the bucket*, *pop off* (corresponding probably more or less to French *s'éteindre*, *décéder*, *mourir*, *casser sa pipe*, *clamser*). Most dictionaries make at least the distinction between « formal » and « informal » (with « soutenu » or « littéraire » on the one hand, and « familier » on the other as the usual equivalents in French), though many propose more subtle differences. Thus the labels used by the Collins English Dictionary, the Longman Dictionary of Contemporary English, the Oxford Advanced Learner's Dictionary, and by the Trésors de la langue française, the Petit Robert and the Dictionnaire du français contemporain are as follows:

CED : informal, slang, taboo
LDCE : formal, not formal, informal, slang, taboo
OALD : rhetorical, formal, informal, slang, offensive

TLF : rhétorique, familier, populaire, argot, vulgaire
PR : littéraire, familier, populaire, vulgaire
DFC : soutenu, littéraire, populaire, argot, trivial

This is how the same dictionaries label some verbs of stealing from the point of view we are concerned with here:

	CED	LDCE	OALD
to purloin	-	formal	formal
to steal	-	-	-
to pilfer	-	-	-
to pinch	informal	informal	informal
to snitch	slang	informal	slang
to swipe	slang	informal	informal

	TLF	PR	DFC
dérober	-	littéraire	soutenu
voler	-	-	-
chaparder	familier	familier	familier
piquer	populaire	populaire	populaire
calotter	argot&pop	populaire	0
chiper	familier	familier	familier

The lack of clear-cut distinctions in this area of linguistic analysis, already referred to above, clearly emerges from these classifications. In passing it may also be worth pointing out that the terms «slang» and «argot» are used both to denote popular or vulgar words such as E. *bloke*, *fag*, F. *mec*, *sèche*(=*man, cigarette*), and to denote the vocabulary used by certain social groups (e. g. E. *grass*, *trip*, F. *herbe*, *trip* in the language of drug users, E. *exams*, *digs*, F. *prof*, *fac* in the language of students).

- The subject matter. If one analyses linguistic forms from the point of view of what is the subject matter of the communication process, many varieties or «registers» may be distinguished: scientific language (with several subvarieties), religious language, poetic language, etc. What characterizes these varieties above all is the specific vocabulary. A few examples:

medical language: E. *scapula*, *abdomen*, *scalpel*
F. *thyroïde*, *thrombose*, *thermocautère*, etc.

legal language: E. *defendant*, *plaintiff*, *injunction*
F. *jurisprudentiel*, *assesseur*, *édicter*, etc.

the language of computing: E. *megabyte*, *diskette*, *cursor*
F. *fichier*, *sauver*, *ligne de format*, etc

religious language: E. *the Lord*, *the Holy Father*, *benediction*
F. *béatitudes*, *tabernacle*, *chanoine*, etc.

poetic language: E. *foe*, *blithe*, *dale*
F. *bocage*, *val*, *onde*, etc.

- The medium used. In culturally developed communities most people are capable of communicating via two media :speech or writing. It is possible, of course, to make use of quite different styles within each of these two systems, so that the language used in a familiar conversation, for instance, may be closer to that of an informal letter than to that of a ceremonious speech. But on the whole it may be said that some vocabulary items tend to occur more frequently in speech, others more often in writing:

	SPEECH	WRITING
E.	*to ask*	*to request*
	to get	*to obtain*
	to buy	*to purchase*
	to need	*to require*
	to look for	*to seek*
	tip	*gratuity*
F.	*rigoler*	*rire*
	gros	*corpulent*
	amusant	*plaisant*
	croissant	*recrudescent*
	sale	*malpropre*
	embêtant	*ennuyeux*

It is clear that even a sketchy classification such as the one presented here poses serious problems. Not only because the « line of demarcation »between styles (between formal and informal, for instance) is a vague one, but also because there is obviously a considerable amount of overlapping. Thus some styles go hand in hand, whereas others exclude each other: religious items will as a rule be formal, whereas non-U items are often informal. It should also be observed that there is a correlation between stylistic meaning and connotative meaning, for the connotation of a word is often responsible for its use in given circumstances, and vice versa.

Linguists sometimes take the term « style » in a wider sense than has so far been suggested. This is the case when not only social status, relationship between users, subject matter and medium are considered, but also the « circumstances » of time and place.

On the basis of the factor of time, Old English will for instance be identified as a variety different from Middle English, or Early Modern English as a variety different from Contemporary English, etc.

The factor of place allows us to distinguish geographical varieties or dialects. Such widespread languages as English and French have to be differentiated into important national varieties (British English, American English, Canadian English, Australian English, Nigerian English, etc.; français de France, de Belgique, de Suisse, du Zaïre, français canadien, etc.), within each of which there may be a great richness of local dialects. Although differences are most marked at the level of pronunciation, specific lexical items are also legion. A few examples are:

American English: *closet* (for British *cupboard*), *fall* (*autumn*), *gas* (*petrol*), *line* (*queue*), *elevator* (*lift*), *truck* (*lorry*), *mail* (*post*), *sidewalk* (*pavement*), *trash* (*rubbish*), *vacation* (*holiday*)

Australian English: *footpath* (*pavement*), *frock* (*dress*), *station* (*ranch*), *sheila* (*girl*), *singlet* (*vest*), *washer* (*face-cloth*)

Belgian French: *doubler une classe* (*redoubler*), *brosser un cours* (*sécher*), *bloquer un cours* (*bûcher, potasser*), *légumier* (*vendeur de légumes*), *pistolet* (*petit pain*) , *ramassette* (*pelle à balai*), *septante* (*soixante-dix*), *nonante* (*quatre-vingt-dix*)

Canadian French: *char* (*automobile*), *boucane* (*fumée*), *touage* (*remorquage*), *vidangeur* (*éboueur*), *vivoir* (*salle de séjour*), *tabagie* (*bureau de tabac*), *magasiner* (*faire ses courses*)

Zaïrian French: *boumer* (*danser*), *campusard* (*étudiant habitant le campus*), *frousser* (*avoir peur*), *humaniste* (*diplômé du secondaire*), *appliquer l'article quinze* (*se débrouiller*).

I. 7. COLLOCATIONAL MEANING

Taken in its wide sense, the linguistic term «collocation» (from Latin «collocatio» = bringing together, grouping) refers to any syntactic combination of words. In this sense E. *pretty flower*, *birds fly*, *drink wine*, *very hot*, F. *grande maison*, *l'oiseau chante*, *viens vite*, *peu enthousiaste* are all collocations.

In this survey we shall take the term in a more limited sense, in fact in the sense of what linguists often call «restrictive collocation». In order to make this sense clear (and to make clear what is meant by «collocational meaning») it is perhaps best to start from a number of combinations which are linguistically unacceptable, and by examining the reasons for the unacceptability, to come to a definition.

Consider the combinations

a1. **(John) laughs his brother*
a2. **(Jean) rit son frère*
bl. **(Paul) refuses come*
b2. **(Paul) refuse venir*

cl. **The dog smiles*
c2. **Le chien sourit*

dl. **(Mary) drinks the bread*
d2. **(Marie) boit le pain*
el. **a blue apple*
e2. **une pomme bleue*

fl. **(It's) turning late*
f2. **(Il) devient tard*
gl. **a large cold*
g2. **un grand rhume*

The combination of the words of a language into a syntactic pattern is subject to certain constraints, which result from the selectional restrictions of these words. These selectional restrictions are of three kinds :grammatical, semantic and usage-determined.

The examples given under a and b represent word combinations which are unacceptable because of the particular grammatical selection restrictions of the verbs *to laugh*, *rire* and *to refuse*, *refuser*. The verbs in al and a2 have a syntactic feature /intransitive/, so that they cannot be combined with a noun in object function. In bl and b2 they are characterized by a grammatical feature which may be presented as /+ marked infinitive/, so that * *refuses come* and * *refuse venir* are to be rejected.

In c, d and e the unacceptability no longer results from grammatical restrictions but from semantic ones. In c the verbs *smile*, *sourire* have a semantic feature /+human subject/, which makes the combinations given unacceptable. In d the combinations are equally unacceptable, because the objects *bread*, *pain* are incompatible with the verbs *to drink*, *boire*, which have a feature /liquid object/. The cases under e also illustrate semantic incompatibility, but whereas the features in c and d apply to whole classes of words (verbs in our examples), the feature /red/ in *apple* is more particular.

With the cases in f and g the problem is quite different. Unacceptability of the word combinations here is due neither to grammatical selection restrictions (for copula + adjective and adjective + noun are perfect English and French syntactic patterns), nor to semantic ones (for the conceptual meaning contents of E. *turn* and *late*, F. *devenir* and *tard*, of E. *large* and *a cold*, F. *grand* and *un rhume* are quite compatible). The constraints or selection restrictions in these cases are merely a matter of usage. It just so happens that the native speaker of English, when he wants to express the concept of « come to be », will select the item *get* or *become* rather than *turn* in combination with the adjective *old*; similarly, he will prefer the adjective *bad* to other « synonymous » adjectives in combination with the noun *cold*. Mutatis mutandis, considerations of the same order can be made with regard to F. **devenir tard* (for *se faire tard*) and **grand rhume* (for *gros rhume*).

Collocation is the term we shall now use both for the linguistic phenomenon whereby a given vocabulary item prefers the company of another item rather than that of its « synonyms » because of constraints which are not on the level of syntax or conceptual meaning but on that of usage, as also for the word combinations which represent this phenomenon. Collocational meaning then is the meaning of a word as far as it is determined by the lexical company it keeps. E. *get old*, *bad cold*, F. *se faire vieux*, *gros rhume* are collocations, and the fact that *get* is preferred as a copula with *old*, *turn* as a copula with e. g. *red*, *go* with *mad* etc. is part of the total meaning of *get*, *turn* and *go* :more precisely, it constitutes their collocational meaning. It would indeed be impossible to explain the difference between these adjectives without referring to the phenomena of co-occurrence which characterize them.

Let us turn to some more examples in both English and French:

E. *wide* and *broad* both denote « measuring a good deal from side to side ». With many nouns they are freely interchangeable (*a wide river a broad river*, *a wide street a broad street*, *a wide margin a broad margin*), but there is preferential selection and therefore collocation in e. g. *wide trousers*, *a wide door*, and in *broad shoulders*, *a broad face*;

E. *to direct*, *to manage*, *to run*, *to conduct*, *to lead* all express « to regulate or control the affairs of » (=F. diriger). However, few nouns freely combine in object function with several or all of these verbs. Some collocations are :*to direct an operation*, *to manage/run a company*, *to lead a party*, *to conduct an orchestra*;

F. *frais*, *coûts*, *dépenses*, *charges* are interchangeable in many contexts, but not in e. g. *frais de déplacement*, *coûts de production*, *charges du loyer*, which are collocations;

F. *donner*, *accorder*, *octroyer*, *concéder*, *allouer* are conceptually synonymous, but collocations are numerous :*donner une aumône*, *accorder une faveur*, *octroyer des lettres de noblesse*, *concéder des privilèges*, *allouer une pension* are a few examples.

Some vocabulary items are very exclusive in the lexical company they keep. This is the case, for instance, with the adjectives E. *addled*, *rancid*, *ruddy*, *blond* or *sleek*, and F. *ouvrable*, *diluvien*, *échéant*, *bée* or *aquilin*. They occur in only one or two combinations:

addled egg	*jour ouvrable*
rancid butter/bacon	*pluie diluvienne*
ruddy face/cheeks	*cas échéant*

blond hair	*bouche bée*
sleek hair/fur	*nez aquilin..*

Because of the frequent association and the interdependence of the two elements, such combinations come close to compounds on the one hand (E. *greenhouse*, *stronghold*, F. *bas-bleu*, *coffre-fort*), to idioms on the other hand (E. *to kick the bucket*, *to pull someone's leg*, *to spill the beans*, F. *passer l'arme à gauche*, *mettre quelqu'un en boîte*, *mettre les pieds dans le plat*). But there are clear differences. First of all, the constitutive elements of compounds and idioms form one inseparable lexical item, which is not the case for close or exclusive collocations (E. *rancid or fresh butter*, *his hair was sleek*, F. *un nez presqu'aquilin*, *la pluie était diluvienne*). Secondly, the total meaning of idioms and often also of compounds cannot be derived from the meanings of the individual words they contain, which is the case with collocations, even when exclusive.

The line between conceptual and collocational meaning is not always easy to draw. Some would probably claim that if, in the case of adjectives denoting « gone rotten or bad », *rancid«* is preferred to other items in combination with *butter*, this is because there is a specific kind of « rottenness » of butter, different from that of eggs or apples for instance. Here semanticists are on very unsure ground. But surely in many cases no such claim can be made. To take only the case of *blond*: as Palmer puts it (1981, 76), « we should not talk about **a blond door* or a **a blond dress*, even if the colour were exactly that of blond hair ». On the other hand it is of course clear that the restrictions on the combinatory possibilities of lexical items may be partially conceptual, partially collocational. The uses of *to make* and *to do*, for instance, can be accounted for conceptually in *to make a box* and *to do good* by saying that *to make* means « to bring into existence by construction and elaboration »(OED) and *to do* « perform, execute »(ibid.). But *to make the beds* and *to do the rooms* can only be explained collocationally.

Because collocation is a matter of individual characteristics of words, where ipso facto no generalizations can be made and where no rules can be laid down, it causes the greatest difficulties in foreign language learning and teaching, the more so as it is also a much neglected aspect of word meaning in dictionaries.

I. 8. CHANGE OF MEANING

For language to function adequately as a means of communication in society it is necessary that the meanings of words should have a high degree of stability. *Father*, *mother*, *life*, *death*, *sun*, *moon*, *wind* and *sea* are only a few examples of the many English lexical items which have for centuries denoted what they denote today, and many more recent, technical items (*radio*, *biology*, *telephone*, *molecule*, *neutron*, etc.) are not likely to change their meaning in the near future. On the other hand, however, society should also be able to adapt its communication system to changing circumstances and to new requirements, which will lead to the creation of new words but also to changes in the meanings of existing ones.

From a conceptual point of view the fact that a word changes its meaning may imply 1° that it loses its original meaning and replaces it by a new one, or 2° that it adds a new meaning to the existing one(s). Examples of the former phenomenon are E. *stool* (originally «chair», now only a particular type of chair :F. *tabouret*) and F. *danger* (originally used in the sense of «pouvoir» , now in that of «péril»); the latter phenomenon may be illustrated by E. *leg* (of the body, of a table, etc.) or F. *feuille* (d'un arbre, de papier, etc.).

Classifying the different types of semantic change is not an easy task, partly because of the difficulty of making a distinction between the nature and the cause of change. Stern (1931) and Ullmann(1962) have proposed intricate classifications, but we prefer to make a basic distinction between non-figurative change and figurative change , i. e. between shift of meaning and transfer of meaning.

A. Shift of meaning: This term may cover various subtypes, the most common ones of which are:

- functional shift occurs when the «thing meant» or referent has itself changed. Thus E. *holiday* , *pen* and *wife* originally meant respectively «religious festival», «feather» and «woman»; F. *rosaire*, *pavillon* and *secrétaire* respectively «guirlande de roses», «tente» and «confident, dépositaire de secrets»;

- narrowing or specialisation of meaning may be observed in e. g. E. *meat* (originally used in the sense of «food»), *deer* (originally «animal»), *undertaker* (originally «contractor»); F. *viande* went through the same narrowing as E. *meat*, whereas *passager* in the 16th century referred to «personne qui prend passage à bord d'un navire», and *épice* was used in the sense of «denrée»;

- widening or generalisation of meaning: E. *bird* once meant «young bird», *picture* was used with reference only to a painted representation of something, *to sail* only with reference to sailboats; F. *boucher* once denoted only «celui qui abat les boucs», *panier* only «corbeille à pain», *arriver* «toucher à la rive».

B. Transfer of meaning or «figurative sense» involves a more marked referential change. Two varieties are traditionally distinguished: metaphor and metonymy.

In the case of metaphor a given lexical item is used to denote a referent (the «tenor») which is in some way similar to the one it basically denotes (the «vehicle»). This is an extremely productive device in language, which may be of occasional, individual use (in the language of poets, for instance, but also in popular speech), but of which there are lots of institutionalised cases. The following are only a few examples, but sufficient , by the way, to show that different languages may of course use different metaphors:

E. *the foot of a mountain* :	F. *le pied d'une montagne*
the arm of a chair :	*le bras d'un fauteuil*
the eye of a needle :	*l'oeil/le chas d'une aiguille*
the head of a nail :	*la tête d'un clou*
an elastic rule :	*une règle élastique*
a warm voice :	*une voix chaude*
a cold welcome :	*un accueil froid*
a meagre salary :	*un salaire maigre*
a broken man :	*un homme brisé*
to break the silence :	*rompre le silence*
the spine of a book :	*le dos d'un livre*
a ray of hope :	*une lueur d'espoir*
the leg of a table :	*le pied d'une table*
sick humor :	*humour noir*
to shoulder a responsibility :	*endosser une responsabilité.*

As may be seen also, the similarity may in some cases be called objective, either physically (*eye*, *leg*, ...) or functionally (*foot*, *arm*, ...), whereas in other cases it will be merely psychological or emotive (*warm*, *cold*, ...).

In some cases the language user is no longer aware of the original reference, as with *talent*, originally a weight of gold or silver, or *crane* (F. *grue*), originally a bird. The metaphor is then said to be «dead».

In the case of metonymy a given lexical item is used to denote a referent other than the one it basically denotes, not because of similarity, but because of an association between the two. Such associations may be of many different types and change of meaning through metonymy is therefore an extremely current phenomenon and a very frequent source of polysemy. The three meanings of E. *government* or F. *gouvernement*, for example, are to be explained by metonymy:

1. The activity of governing (*The young prince had no talent for government*);

2. The form or method of carrying out this activity (*Democratic governement has been taken for granted in this country for centuries*);

3. The group of people who carry out this activity (*The government are discussing the proposal*).

Some well-known types of metonymy are:

- the word denoting part of something is used to denote the whole («pars pro toto»): E. *a redcap, he is the brain of the school, all hands on deck!*, F. *un blouson noir, une forte tête, le toit paternel*;

- the whole to denote a part («totum pro parte») is much less frequent: E. *the dome of a church*, in sport: *Scotland beat Wales*, F. *elle s'est offert un vison, un sac en crocodile*;

- the container denotes the content: E. *he's too fond of the bottle, the kettle is boiling, the whole house was woken up*, F. *boire un verre, toute la tribune est debout, sa nouvelle garde-robe*;

- the name of a person to denote the time at which he lived: E. *before Christ, after Cromwell*, F. *après César, avant Louis XIV*, the thing he invented: *watt, volt, macadam, colt, boycott, sandwich*, F. *bottin, calepin, poubelle, mansarde, barème, béchamel, silhouette*, an article of clothing he or she wore: *mackintosh, cardigan, raglan*, F. *cravate, gilet, pantalon*, the work he produced: E. *a beautiful Van Dyck*, F. *un Picasso*, a person with the characteristic he personifies: E. *an Adonis, a Judas, a mentor*, F. *un cerbère, un mécène, un espiègle*;

- the name of a place to denote what is produced or found in it: *tweed, jersey, havana, sherry, bikini, cashmere, champagne, cognac, bordeaux, beaujolais, astrakan*..

I. 9. POLYSEMY AND HOMONYMY

In communication systems in general -in the morse code or in computer language, for instance- it is a golden rule that one symbol stands for one and only one meaning, and that a given meaning is invariably represented by one and the same symbol. The fact that natural languages drastically differ from other communication systems in this respect largely accounts for their complexity. They are far from showing this one-to-one correspondence, for similar (if not identical) meanings are often expressed by two or more forms and, conversely, most word forms represent more than one meaning. The former phenomenon is known as « synonymy », the latter is traditionally either treated as a case of polysemy (caused by the types of semantic change surveyed in I. 8 above) or homonymy. This section will be devoted to a brief discussion of two problems: 1° When is it justified to claim that one linguistic form corresponds to two or more different meanings, as we do both in the case of polysemy and homonymy?

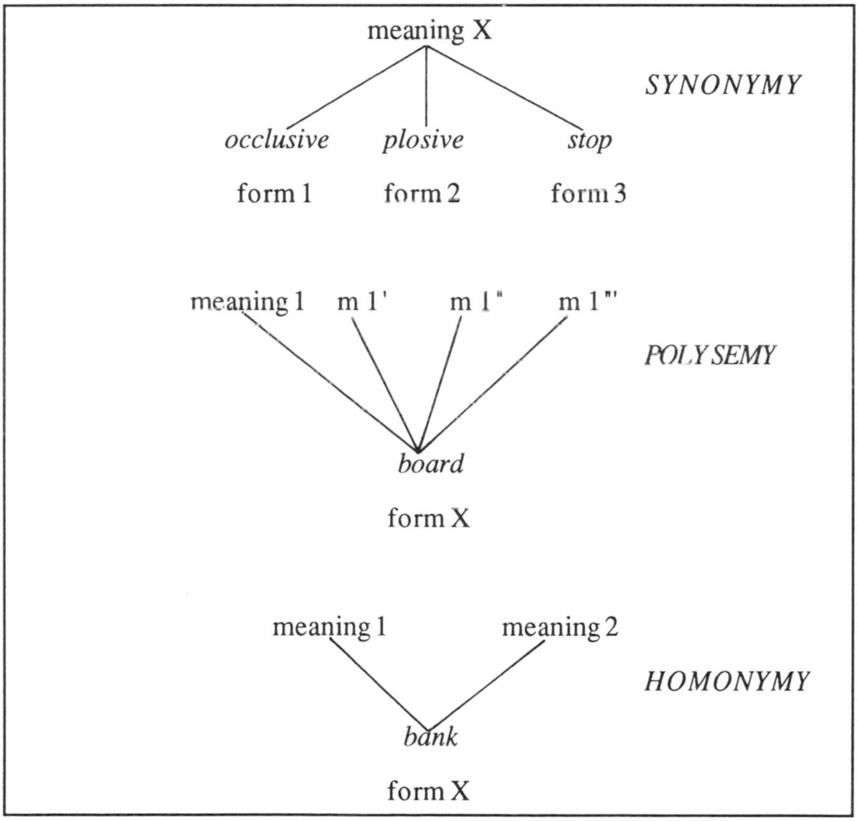

2° What are the criteria that will enable us to distinguish between polysemy and homonymy?

With regard to the first question it is clear that no linguist would think of proposing as many senses for the words *red* and *rouge* as there are shades of this colour, or as many senses for the words *watch* and *montre* as there are types of this particular object. On the other hand not only all linguists, but all speakers of English and French are likely to agree that *hard* and *dur* or *canon* and *canon* each have more than one sense. Linguists (Benvéniste, Dubois, Cowie, Cruse and others) have been concerned with this serious problem, and the following are some of the criteria they have proposed for diagnosing semantic difference. One form corresponds to different meanings when

1° it has different synonyms and antonyms:

synonyms: E. *match* = contest
match = lucifer
F. *mal* = tort
mal = difficulté

antonyms: E. a *light* bag = a *heavy* bag
a *light* colour = a *dark* colour
a *light* wind = a *strong* wind
light music = *classical* music
F. eau *douce* = eau *salée*
peau *douce* = peau *dure*
musique *douce* = musique *bruyante*
une pente *douce* = une pente *raide*

This criterion, however, has no absolute validity. The synonym test does not apply to E. *crawl* for instance, which has two different senses (cfr. *there's an insect crawling up your sleeve* and *the sight of snakes makes my flesh crawl*) but *creep* as a synonym in both cases. Neither does it apply to F. *manquer* (cfr. *manquer son train* and *manquer une photo*), with *rater* as a synonym in its two senses. The same holds true for the antonym test:E. *light* has *heavy* as an antonym in both *a light bag* and *a light duty*, F. *doux* has the antonym *dur* in both *une peau douce* and *un doux regard*.

2° it has different compounds or derivations:

E. *mine*: *miner*, *coalmine*, *goldmine*
mine: *minefield*, *minesweeper*

drive:*driver*, *drive-in*
drive:*drift* (of snow)

tend: *(bar-) tender*
tend: *tendency*

F. *fumer*: *fumeur*, *fumoir*
fumer: *fumage*, *fumée*

gauche: *gaucher*
gauche: *gauchiste*

propre: *propreté*, *malpropre*
propre: *propriété*, *impropre*

Apart from the fact that this criterion applies only to part of the vocabulary (for E. *lilt* or F. *tympan*, for instance, lack compound and derived forms in both their senses), there are also counterexamples (E. *hard* has *harden* and *hardness*, F. *discret* has *discrétion* and *discrètement* in at least two senses).

3° it enters into different syntactic patterns:

With nouns, the opposition countable/uncountable as a rule implies a semantic distinction (E. *a stone*:*stone*, F. *un verre, du verre*).

With verbs, the opposition transitive/intransitive is in itself often insufficient to speak of difference in meaning (E. *to sing a song*:*to sing*, F. *lire un livre*:*lire*), except, for instance, when this opposition coincides with thedistinction causative/non-causative (E. *he broke the window, the window broke*, F. *il brûle le papier, le papier brûle*).

Different types of subject or object and, at a deeper level, different «participant roles» will also be formal indications of distinctions of meaning. Thus the analysis of E. *to assemble* and F. *appréhender* leads to the discovery of two senses:

assemble (a team):	subject: human, role: actor object: human, role: affected
assemble (a bookcase):	subject: human, role: actor object: inanimate, role: effected
appréhender (un danger):	subject: human, role: experiencer object: inanimate, role: source
appréhender (un voleur):	subject: human, role: actor object: human, role: affected

4° it is the source of puns. This is of course of limited practicability as a test, but it is true that puns are generally based on plurality of sense. Thus the oddness or humour of apparently contradictory utterances such as *être à cheval sur un âne*, *débarquer d'un train* or *atterrir sur la lune* is due to the extension of the meaning of one of the forms they contain. The typical humour of the Belgian entertainer Raymond Devos is largely based on this. Consider also the following puns, some of which have been taken from Cruse (1982, 73), some from other sources:

John and his licence expired last Thursday
He swallowed my story and the drink I offered him
We were left with 500 pairs of boots on our hands

Qui a bu trinquera
Quand les parents boivent, les enfants trinquent
Il faut une armoire à glace pour déplacer ce frigo

Les femmes vous aimeront encore mieux quand elles ne pourront plus vous sentir (commercial for a deodorant)

Obviously, while these criteria may be helpful, they have only relative value and, moreover, they do not allow us to distinguish polysemy from homonymy, a problem we will now briefly examine.

A word is said to be polysemous when it has two or more meanings which are related to each other. As a look at the dictionary shows, practically all lexical words are of this type, and, in a general way, the more frequent a word is, the more polysemous it tends to be. Thus the words denoting parts of the body (E. *head*, *foot*, *eye*, *hand*, F. *tête*, *bras*, *pied*, ...), for instance, are all used in many different acceptations. Some items are polysemous to the extent that they have almost become senseless «passe-partout» words: The Oxford English Dictionary lists 34 «meanings» for the verb *to get* (with further sub-meanings in many cases), and the Trésor de la langue française lists almost as many for *aller*.

The way one and the same polysemous word is treated in different dictionaries clearly shows that it is often far from easy to decide 1° where one meaning ends and another one starts, i. e. how many meanings should be distinguished, and 2° which of them should be regarded as basic.

The first difficulty should not come as a surprise, of course, after what was said about the fuzzy nature of the concepts we have: more often than not, they cannot be neatly delimited, but are vague and merge into one another. Take the verb *to sing*, for example: should a dictionary maker distinguish two different meanings for this item according to whether reference is made to a person or to a bird, two different kinds of phenomenon, to be sure. (It is interesting to note that the Longman Dictionary of Contemporary English makes the distinction for the noun (*song*), but not for the verb). The comparison of two different treatments of the adjective *poor* and of the French word *région* on the following pages illustrates this delicate problem of cutting up the semantic space covered by a lexical item. Not only does one dictionary distinguish a larger number of senses or subsenses in each case, but some of the shared meanings are not fully identical. There simply is no final criterion by which to decide where one meaning ends and another one begins, but on the whole lexicographers tend to overlook minor differences.

With regard to the order in which the senses of a polysemous item are presented in dictionaries, priority may be given either to the original sense(s) of the word or to the most frequent sense(s) in present-day usage. The two may of course coincide, but this is not necessarily so. Thus the Oxford English Dictionary, which adopts a diachronic point of view, describes the item *pipe* as 1°a musical instrument, 2° a whistle used by boatswains, 3° a tube, 4° an object used for smoking, whereas the Longman Dictionary of Contemporary English has these senses in the order 3°, 4°, 1°, 2°.

RANDOM HOUSE DICTIONARY

poor (po͝or), *adj.* **1.** having little or no money, goods, or other means of support: *a poor family living on welfare.* **2.** *Law.* dependent upon charity or public support. **3.** (of a country, institution, etc.) meagerly supplied or endowed with resources or funds. **4.** characterized by or showing poverty. **5.** deficient or lacking in something specified: *a region poor in mineral deposits.* **6.** faulty or inferior, as in construction: *poor workmanship.* **7.** deficient in desirable ingredients, qualities, or the like: *poor soil.* **8.** lean or emaciated, as cattle. **9.** of an inferior, inadequate, or unsatisfactory kind: *poor health.* **10.** lacking in skill, ability, or training: *a poor cook.* **11.** deficient in moral excellence; cowardly, abject, or mean. **12.** scanty, meager, or paltry in amount or number: *a poor audience.* **13.** humble; modest: *They shared their poor meal with a stranger.* **14.** unfortunate; hapless: *The poor dog was limping.* **15.** **poor as Job's turkey,** extremely poor; impoverished: *They're poor as Job's turkey, but just as proud as they come.* —*n.* **16.** (*construed as pl.*) poor persons collectively (usually prec. by *the*): *sympathy for the poor.* [ME *pov(e)re* < OF *povre* < L *pauper.* See PAUPER] —**poor′ness,** *n.*

COLLINS ENGLISH DICTIONARY

poor (pʊə, pɔː) *adj.* **1. a.** lacking financial or other means of subsistence; needy. **b.** (*as collective n.;* preceded by *the*)*: the poor.* **2.** characterized by or indicating poverty: *the country had a poor economy.* **3.** deficient in amount; scanty or inadequate: *a poor salary.* **4.** (*when postpositive,* usually foll. by *in*) badly supplied (with resources, materials, etc.): *a region poor in wild flowers.* **5.** lacking in quality; inferior. **6.** giving no pleasure; disappointing or disagreeable: *a poor play.* **7.** (*prenominal*) deserving of pity; unlucky: *poor John is ill again.* **8.** **poor man's (something).** a (cheaper) substitute for (something). [C13: from Old French *povre,* from Latin *pauper;* see PAUPER, POVERTY] —**'poorness** *n.*

PETIT ROBERT

RÉGION [ʀeʒjɔ̃]. *n. f.* (1380; « pays », fin XIe; lat. *regio* « direction; frontière, contrée », de *regere*). ♦ 1° Territoire relativement étendu, possédant des caractères physiques et humains particuliers qui en font une unité distincte des régions voisines ou au sein d'un ensemble qui l'englobe. V. **Contrée, province, zone.** *Régions naturelles. Les régions polaires. Région désolée. Régions cultivées. Région à population dense. Carte d'une région.* ◇ Par ext. *Dans nos régions :* dans nos climats, nos pays. ◇ *Spécialt.* Unité territoriale administrative groupant en France plusieurs départements (V. Circonscription). *Régions militaires.* Absolt. *Le général commandant la région. L'état-major de la région. Régions judiciaires. — Régions maritimes, aériennes.* — (Anc.). *Régions économiques :* en France, Groupements régionaux de chambres de commerce. ♦ 2° Étendue de pays autour d'une ville. *Aller en vacances dans la région de Royan. Parcourir, sillonner la région.* ♦ 3° *Fig.* (de *la région éthérée,* philo. anc.). Domaine, sphère. « *Les hautes régions de la philosophie* » (MOL.). « *Une région supérieure où la joie et la douleur n'existent plus* » (MART. du G.). ♦ 4° (XVIe). Partie, zone déterminée (du corps). *Région lombaire, plantaire, palmaire.* ◇ Fig. « *La région proprement pensante de son être* » (BENDA). *Les régions de la sensibilité.*

LEXIS (LAROUSSE)

RÉGION [reʒjɔ̃] n. f. (lat. *regio,* de *regere,* diriger; v. 1080, « direction »). **1.** (1380). Étendue de pays caractérisée soit par une unité humaine, administrative ou économique, soit par la similitude du relief, du climat, de la végétation : *Une région industrielle, agricole. Comme le soleil d'été dans les régions polaires, la sphère éclatante parut hésiter, puis remonta vers le zénith* (Yourcenar). — **2.** Étendue de pays quelconque : *Visiter la région parisienne. Je lisais toutes les nouvelles contenues dans « l'Écho de Lauingen », et les dates de foires de toute la région* (Giraudoux). — **3.** (v. 1500). Partie du corps plus ou moins arbitrairement délimitée : *Région cervicale, pectorale.* — **4.** Circonscription territoriale militaire, terrestre, aérienne ou maritime, englobant plusieurs départements et commandée par un officier général. — **5.** *Ch. de f.* Chacune des divisions administratives remplaçant les anciens réseaux. — **6.** *Math.* Partie du plan limitée par des droites ou des courbes; partie de l'espace limitée par des plans ou des surfaces. — **7.** Point où l'on s'élève dans certaines sciences : *C'est un esprit spéculatif qui se plaît dans les plus hautes régions de la philosophie* (syn. SPHÈRE). — **8.** *Bot.* Massif de cellules séparé par des limites très nettes. — **9.** *Région économique,* ancienne dénomination des chambres régionales de commerce et d'industrie.

Homonymy, as opposed to polysemy, is the term reserved for cases where one form corresponds to two or more meanings which are semantically unrelated. Whereas cases of polysemy will as a rule be represented by one entry (i.e. as one word) in dictionaries, cases of homonymy will be represented by two (i. e. as two words). Though homonymy is of course less frequent than polysemy, there are plenty of cases in both French and English:

E. *bank* (of a river, from Ital. *banca*)
bank (financial institution, from Old Icel. *bakki*)

ball (toy, from Old Norse *böllr*)
ball (dance, from Latin *ballare*)

bat (club used e. g. in baseball, from Celtic *bat*)
bat (mouselike nocturnal animal, from Scand. *batta*)

F. *vase* (récipient, from Lat. *vas*)
vase (boue, from Middle Dutch *wase*)

son (bruit, from Latin *sonus*)
son (résidu de la mouture des grains, from medieval Latin *seonno*)

louer (glorifier, from Latin *laudare*)
louer (donner/prendre à loyer, from Latin *locare*)

In a strict sense the term «homonymy» is used for pairs of words whose written and spoken forms are identical, as in the examples just given. The term «homophones» is then used for items which only share their spoken form, as is the case with E. *to sow* and *to sew*, *night* and *knight*, or French *fin* and *faim*, *compte*, *comte* and *conte*, whereas «homographs» refers to identical spelling forms but different phonetic shapes, as in E. *bow* and *bow*, *primate* and *primate*, or F. *(nous) portions* and *(les) portions*. The term «partial homonymy» is occasionally used for pairs of identical form belonging to different word classes, as E. *last* (adjective) and *last* (verb), *ring* (noun) and *ring* (verb), or F. *son* (possessive determiner) and *son* (noun), *boucher* (noun) and *boucher* (verb), *portions* (noun) and *portions* (of the verb *porter*).

The criterion of «unrelatedness of meaning», which is used to distinguish homonymy from polysemy, does not raise a problem in the examples given so far. In addition, the marked difference in meaning usually goes hand in hand with a different etymology (cfr. the different origins of *bank* and *bank*, *vase* and *vase* etc. in the examples above), so that in practice this is often considered and used as an objective criterion. It is not always reliable, however, for some pairs of different origin have developed meanings which are relatively close, as in

E. *mean* (average) and *mean* (low, ignoble), respectively from Latin *medianus* and *(com)munis*

F. *bourse* (petit sac à argent) and *bourse* (lieu où se font des opérations financières), respectively from Latin *bursa* and the Dutch name *Van der Burse.*

Conversely, some meanings which do not seem related go back to one and the same origin, as in

E. *crane* (kind of bird) and *crane* (machine for lifting), both from Old English *cran*

fast (quick) and *fast* (firm), both going back to Old English *faest*

sole (underside of the foot) and *sole* (fish), both via Old French from Latin *solea*

F. *grue* and *grue* (see E. *crane*)

voler (E. steal) and *voler* (E. fly), both from Latin*volare*. The sense «steal» was derived from the sense «chasser en volant», speaking of birds of prey

grève (E. strike) and *grève* (E. shore, bank), both from *Place de Grève*, on the bank of the Seine, where striking Parisian workers used to assemble in the 18th century

cor (ramification du bois des cerfs;instrument de musique) and *cor* (au pied), both from Latin *cornu.*

Because of these difficulties in clearly distinguishing homonymy and polysemy and neatly delimiting difference of meaning, some semanticists prefer not to distinguish the two phenomena and to see the different meanings corresponding to single forms as part of a continuum ranging from «almost identical» to «completely different».

It might seem that polysemy and homonymy are in fact a weakness of the linguistic system. In one sense they are, of course, as they may give rise to ambiguity in communication (as in E. *She cannot bear children* or in F. *Il s'est acheté une glace*). But this is rarely the source of real problems, for linguistic context and/or the speech situation usually compensate for this theoretical difficulty. In fact, polysemy and homonymy are clearly a great factor of economy in natural languages, for it enables human beings to cope with the infinitude of their entire world of experience by means of a limited number of lexical elements. If we needed a different word for each of the thousands and thousands of meanings and shades of meaning we may wish to express, and if we could not express new meanings with existing words, language would not be the manageable code it is now.

CHAPTER II: THE STRUCTURE OF THE LEXICON

Analysing the meaning of individual words is only part of the lexicologist's task. Studying the relations of meaning which hold between words and groups of words, and examining to what extent the vocabulary as a whole can be seen as an interrelated system is also part of his task. Linguists in the past concentrated mainly on individual lexical items and especially on the historical development of their forms (i. e. on etymology), but since structuralists insisted on the fact that linguistic forms are not to be considered as isolated, independent elements, but form a system of relations and oppositions «où tout se tient»(de Saussure), lexicologists have been more concerned with the lexicon as a system of meaning relations. However, for reasons already stated (Introduction, I), progress has been much slower on the level of the lexicon than on the levels of phonology and grammar.

In this chapter we intend to deal first of all with the notion of lexical fields and, more particularly, semantic fields, and with the technique of componential analysis, both of which are currently used by semanticists with a view to discovering relations between words and groups of words. Next we shall survey the different types of meaning relations which are traditionally distinguished in lexicology.

II. 1. SEMANTIC FIELDS

The words of the vocabulary are in association with other words in different ways. Thus the Swiss structuralist F. de Saussure pointed out in his «Cours de linguistique générale» (1915) that the French word *enseignement* has associative relations with *enseigner*, *enseignons* etc. because of a common base but different inflectional morphemes, with *apprentissage*, *éducation* etc. because of a common meaning content, with *changement*, *armement* etc. because of a common derivational element (the suffix *-ment*), and with *clément*, *justement* etc. simply because of a common sound sequence (written as *-ment*).

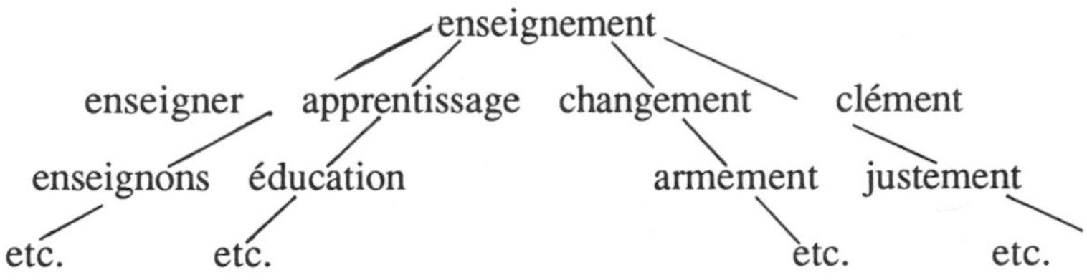

The different types of association have been the basis for different types of linguistic fields, such as Bally's «champs associatifs», Guiraud's «champs morpho-sémantiques», or Matoré's «champs notionnels». It is of course semantic fields (groupings of the type *enseignement*, *apprentissage*, *éducation*) that will be of particular interest to us -and that pose the most difficult problems.

Semantic fields are formed by groups of words more or less closely related in meaning, such as the words referring to beauty, to temperature, to kinship, to colour, to cooking, etc. Duchacek's «champ de la beauté» (as represented by Geckeler, 1973) and Mounin's «champ zoologique» (1972), shown on the following pages, are two illustrations of such field representations.

The study of semantic fields aims at examining the relationships between such words (e. g. synonymy, antonymy, hyponymy) as well as between connected fields, in order to get a better insight into the structure of some parts of the vocabulary. The study of such fields is indeed very valuable in lexicological research, for the meaning of a word can often only be delineated with precision if we compare it with the meaning of other, «neighbouring» words. What *fake* means will only be fully grasped if we compare its semantic content with that of *false*, *counterfeit*, *bogus*, *sham* etc. Again, as de Saussure pointed out, the vocabulary of a language is not an unordered collection of words, but (to some extent at least, some would claim) a structured system, in which the meaning of one item is delimited by the meanings of other, related words.

The first linguist to propose an actual theory of semantic fields was J. Trier(1934). His theory suggests that two planes or continua can be distinguished: the plane of words (the vocabulary) and the plane of concepts or meanings. To each word of the vocabulary corresponds a concept; each word combines with other words into a lexical subfield, which in turn combines with other subfields into larger fields, and each of these subfields and fields corresponds to a subarea and area on the plane of concepts. On both planes these fields and areas fit neatly into each other, without leaving gaps and without overlaps, as do the little stones of a mosaic or the little pieces of a jigsaw puzzle.

Trier's ideas have given rise to much debate. First of all they raise the problem of the relationship between language and thought. Most linguists and psychologists, as will be remembered (see I. 4. 10), reject the strong version of the Whorfian hypothesis, according to which our thinking and our view of the world is entirely determined by the language we speak. But on the other hand most of them also reject the existence of a conceptual continuum totally independent of language, as suggested by Trier's theory. It is now generally believed that conceptualisation is partially determined by the language we speak, partially independent of it.

A second objection concerns the claim that lexical fields are made up of neatly fitting items, without gaps or overlaps. It is clear that all vocabularies leave «conceptual gaps»: as we have seen (I. 4. 10), all languages have words to express certain concepts which are lacking in the vocabularies of other languages, and the blank squares in Mounin's «champ zoologique» are relatively large in number. Overlapping is also a relatively frequent phenomenon, as the number of synonyms or near-synonyms in languages clearly indicates. (See, for instance, *porcelet* and *cochonnet*, *porc* and *cochon* in Mounin's «champ»).

Trier also assumes that lexical fields are closed, clearly delimited sets. This may be so in some areas of reference where reality itself is clearly structured, such as military ranks or kinship terms. But with regard to more abstract and vague areas, such as words connected with beauty, words for sounds and noises or terms of moral evaluation, it may be quite a difficult task to decide which words belong or do not belong to the particular field. To take Duchacek's analysis, it may be questioned whether such items as *gentil*, *aimable*, *délicat* or *idéal* belong to the field of beauty, whereas on the other hand the total absence of antonyms (words for «laideur») impoverishes his analysis of this area of the French vocabulary. (The fact that it is based on out of date sources and does not reflect contemporary French usage we shall disregard here). Mounin himself has pointed out how the seemingly simple field of domestic animals may take on different shapes according to the definition accepted for «domestic animal»: if the characteristic «living in the home of man», given by some dictionaries, is accepted, the fly would have to be included.

Furthermore, Trier's insistence that the whole of the vocabulary is an integrated and fully structured system of fields and subfields cannot be taken seriously. True enough, the field approach has been widely used in studies of word semantics, but most convincingly in areas of relatively simple structure (colour words, words for family relationship, words for military ranks have been favourite sets), and it is far from giving an insight into the total structure of the vocabulary. As Guiraud (1979, 91) puts it, «Il est clair qu'en dehors de(ces)quelques exceptions, on ne saurait confondre la notion de *champ* sémantique avec celle de système phonologique ou morphologique dans lequel chacun des éléments est nécessaire au fonctionnement de l'ensemble et qui seul mérite le nom de «structure»;le champ sémantique est bien un ensemble de relations d'où chaque terme tire sa motivation, mais non nécessaires et non systématiques. Ce caractère contingent des relations lexicales semble interdire tout espoir de ramener le lexique à un système entièrement structuré».

Le champ zoologique

Nom spécifique	Ane	Cheval	Mulet	Bœuf	Chèvre	Mouton	Porc Cochon	Chat	Chien	Lapin	Poule	Canard
Mâle	âne	*étalon*	mulet	*taureau*	*bouc*	*bélier*	*verrat*	chat	chien	lapin	*coq*	canard
Femelle	ânesse	*jument*	mule	*vache*	chèvre	*brebis*	*truie*	chatte	chienne	lapine	poule	cane
Jeune	ânon	*poulain*		*veau*	chevreau	*agneau*	porcelet cochonnet	chaton	chiot	lapereau	poulet	caneton
Parturition		*pouliner*		*vêler*	chevreter	*agneler*	cochonner	chatonner	chienner	lapiner		
Portée							cochonnée	*portée*	*portée*	*portée* *nichée*	*couvée*	*couvée*
Gardien spécifique	ânier		muletier	bouvier	chevrier	*berger*	porcher					
Local d'élevage		*écurie*	*écurie*	bouverie *étable* *vacherie*	*étable*	*bergerie*	*toit* *soue* porcherie cochonnier		chenil *niche*	lapinière *clapier*	poulailler	poulailler
Cri spécifique	*braire*	*hennir*		*mugir* *meugler* *beugler*	*bêler* *chevroter*	*bêler*	*grogner*	*miauler*	*aboyer*	*clapir* *couiner*	*glousser* *caqueter*	*cancaner* *nasiller*

(Mounin, 1972)

La répartition du champ conceptuel de la beauté du point de vue des contenus sémantiques de ses membres

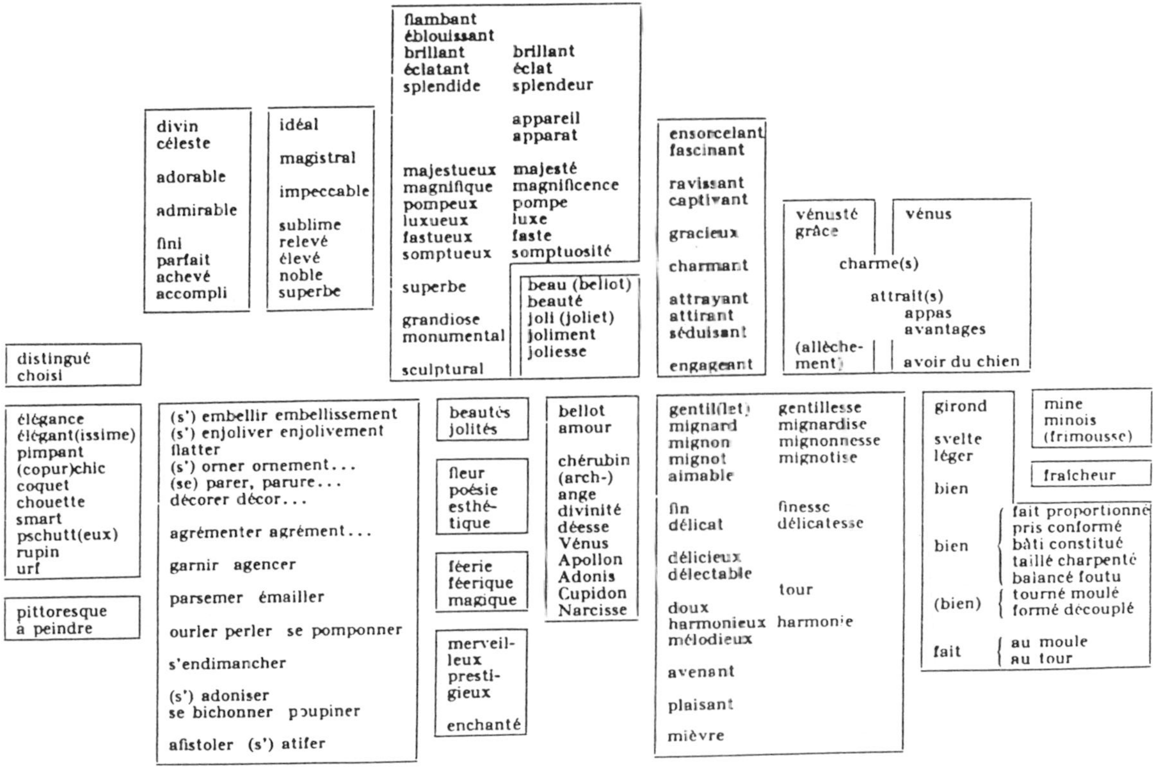

(Geckeler, 1973)

Finally, it is clear that the study of semantic fields does not do justice to word meaning in its totality. If it throws light on the paradigmatic relations (synonymy, near-synonymy, hyponymy) into which related items enter, it does not, for instance, account for the syntagmatic relations, i. e. for the meaning of words in so far as it is determined by their combinability with other words.

In spite of its limitations, in some way or other the field approach has always been and will always be common practice in lexical semantics, in the sense that the comparison of the meanings of related words makes an indispensable contribution to a clearer insight into the meaning content of each of these words.

II. 2. COMPONENTIAL ANALYSIS

Componential analysis, as was shown in I. 4. 4, represents an attempt to break down the conceptual meaning of a lexical item into minimal distinctive features. It is clear that this will enable the linguist to define more economically and more precisely what the relations are between words and groups of words which belong to the same or a related semantic field. Thus, in the field of French «siège» words referred to in I. 4. 4. , componential analysis reveals exactly what elements of meaning respectively link and differentiate the items *chaise*, *fauteuil*, *canapé* etc. Similarly, it will reveal that the groups of words

man	*bull*	*stallion*
woman	*cow*	*mare*
child	*calf*	*foal*

are related in the English vocabulary by the same oppositional structure, which is expressed in terms of the components /male/ and /adult/. Furthermore, such basic semantic relations as synonymy, hyponymy and incompatibility (see below, II. 3) can now be defined with greater accuracy: *Dad* is a conceptual synonym of *father* because it contains the same components, *cat* is a hyponym of *animal* because all the features of *animal* are contained in *cat*, *calf* is incompatible with *foal* because the two items share some features but differ from each other by some other features.

In fact, as Katz and Fodor (1963) have shown, componential analysis can also be used to analyse the relations between the different meanings of a polysemic word, as represented by

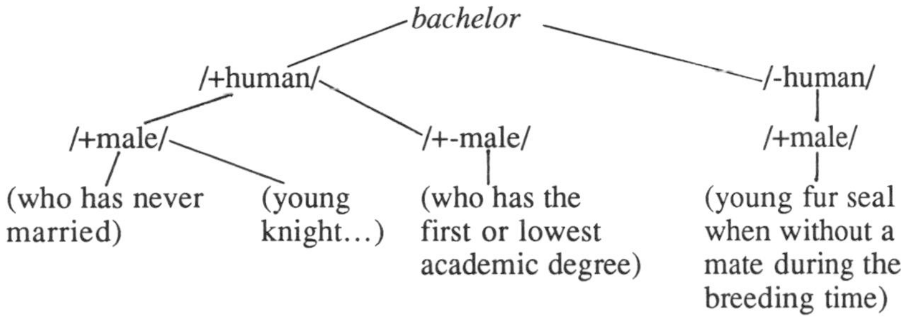

The analysis (whereby components are seen either as « markers », i. e. more basic features such as /human/, /male/, etc. or as « distinguishers », i. e. more specific features, here placed in round brackets) shows that three of the four conceptual meanings of the word *bachelor* are linked by a common feature (/+human/), and that, in turn, two of these three share the feature /+male/.

But the shortcomings and weaknesses of componential analysis were discussed at some length in I. 4. 5, so that the limits of its applicability need not again be emphasized.

II. 3. MEANING RELATIONS BETWEEN WORDS

The relations which exist between the meanings of words are basically of two kinds: paradigmatic and syntagmatic.

Paradigmatic relations hold between words belonging to the same paradigm, i.e. between words which can be substituted for each other in a sequence or, put differently, which can take up the same position in a construction. This implies that paradigmatic relations are relations between words which all belong to the same word class (nouns, verbs, adjectives, etc.). Thus, for instance, *president*, *secretary*, *member* all belong to the same paradigm, as they can all be substituted for each other in the sentence *We talked to the new president of the association.* In the same way, and with the same sentence in mind, the items *new*, *former*, *first*, etc. belong to the same paradigm, as do *talked to*, *spoke to*, *called*, *questioned*, etc.

Syntagmatic relations are relations between words in linear combination, i. e. between words combined with each other in a syntactic construction. Between *new* and *president*, for instance, in the example just given.

Other terms are sometimes used to refer to these two types of semantic relations. Paradigmatic relations can be said to be relations « in absentia », but are also called « substitutional ». Syntagmatic relations are relations «in praesentia» and are also referred to as «combinatorial».

II. 3.1. Paradigmatic relations of meaning

The meaning relations traditionally distinguished between members of the same paradigm are synonymy, hyponymy, incompatibility, and antonymy. This implies that the meanings of words belonging to the same paradigm can either be the same, or partially overlapping, or simply different, or opposed to each other, though actual analysis may reveal relations of a more intricate nature than is suggested by this rough classification.

1° Synonymy

If the term «synonymy» is taken in a strict sense, viz. as the relation that holds between words which have identical meanings and are therefore interchangeable in all contexts and in all situations, then it can hardly be applied to any pair or group of words in any language. Consider the following pairs of words, which one may find described as synonyms by the authors of dictionaries:

a. E. *to answer*:*to reply*,	F. *répondre*:*répliquer*
b. E. *skinny*:*slim*,	F. *maigre*:*mince*
c. E. *salt*:*sodium chloride*,	F. *sel*:*chlorure de sodium*
d. E. *to become*:*to grow*,	F. *devenir*:*se faire*

It is clear that there is no absolute synonymy in any of these cases. In a. the divergence is conceptual: one can *answer a call*, but not **reply a call*, as one may *répondre «oui»*, but not **répliquer «oui»*. In b. there is a connotational difference: whereas *slim* and *mince* may be taken as a compliment by the addressee when referring to his or her physical appearance, *skinny* and *maigre* would probably not be. In c. the members of the pairs belong to different styles, as *sodium chloride* and *chlorure de sodium* are scientific terms. In d. there is a collocational difference: *to become a pilot*, but not **to grow a pilot*, and *devenir fou*, but not **se faire fou*. «Synonymy» is therefore to be taken in the wider sense of the relation that holds between words with approximately the same meaning and, more particularly, with approximately the same conceptual meaning. In this sense most words of the vocabulary have several synonyms, and some (e. g. E. *take* or F. *prendre*) have very many.

As most words also have more than one meaning, synonymy is as a rule limited to one of the meanings of words. Thus E. *hard* is a synonym of *difficult* in *a hard question*, but not in *hard ice*;F. *pointu* is synonymous with *aigu* in *un bec aigu*, but not in *un conflit aigu*..

The fact that absolute synonymy is extremely rare is of course not surprising. It would indeed be a useless luxury, running counter to the principle of economy in language as a communication system. The history of languages has often shown that, when two words have identical meanings (as a result of borrowing, for instance), one of them changes its meaning or simply disappears. Thus, when English borrowed *infant* and *labour* from Middle French, these words were given a sense different from *child* and *work*; when *uncle* and *despair* were borrowed, *eam* and *wanhope* fell into disuse. Similarly, in the French pairs *col* and *cou* (both from Latin *collum*) and *sol* and *sou* (both from Latin *solidus* = « monnaie d'or à valeur fixe » ou « solide »), the two items co-existed for some time with the same meaning, but later *col* and *cou* were semantically differentiated and *sol* disappeared.

2° Hyponymy

Hyponymy or « inclusion » are the terms used to denote a relation whereby the meaning of a word (the « hyponym ») is included in the meaning of another word (the « superordinate term », also « archlexeme »). Thus E. *horse* is a hyponym of *animal*, *to murder* of *to kill*, and *scarlet* of *red*, and the same relation holds between F. *maison* and *bâtiment*, *téléphoner* and *communiquer*, *azur* and *bleu*.. Hyponymy is a case of « unilateral implication », in the sense that one meaning includes the other, but the opposite is not true (a horse is an animal, but the opposite cannot be claimed).

Hyponymy is an important meaning relation, for superordinate terms denote classes, and, as we saw when dealing with semantic fields, it is tempting to see the vocabulary of a language as an organisation of groups and subgroups of words covering fields and subfields of meaning relating to classes and subclasses of « things ». This is suggested by, for example,

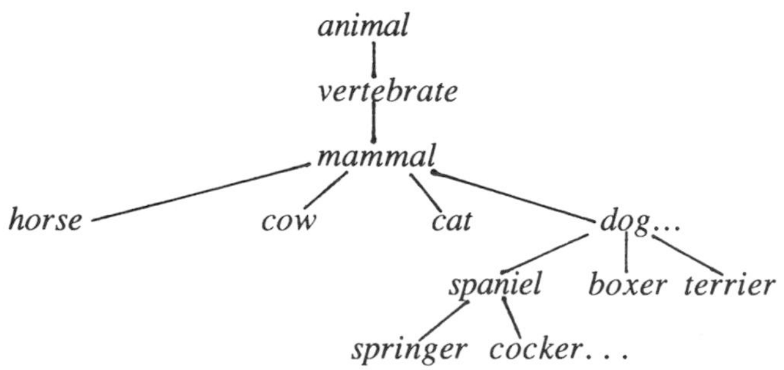

However, not all groups of related words have a superordinate term. There is no English or French vocabulary item that includes

uncle and *aunt*, *oncle* and *tante*, for instance. Nor is there one that includes all colour words, for the terms E. *coloured* and F. *colorié* usually exclude *black*, *white*, and even *grey*, F. *noir*, *blanc* and *gris*.

In the case of polysemous words one meaning may be generic and therefore superordinate to another meaning. This applies to E. *man* and F. *homme*, as well as to some animal words which refer to the species in one sense and to the male (more rarely to the female) in another sense:

man	*homme*
man woman child	*homme femme enfant*
dog	*chien*
dog bitch pup	*chien chienne chiot*
duck	*canard*
drake duck duckling	*canard cane caneton*
goose	*oie*
gander goose gosling	*jars oie oison*

3° Incompatibility

Lexical items are said to be incompatible when they belong to the same general area of meaning, i. e. to the same semantic field, and exclude each other. The colour terms, for instance, are incompatible: if a hat is *red*, it cannot be *green* or *blue* or *yellow*. The same relationship holds between such related words as E. *iron*, *lead*, *copper*, *zinc*, etc. , or *to run*, *to march*, *to crawl*, etc. , or F. *français*, *suisse*, *belge*, etc.

In the case of words which do not belong to the same area of meaning, as E. *red* and *small* or F. *tulipe* and *éléphant*, the notion of incompatibility is of little interest. Linguists will then simply prefer to speak of difference in meaning. This does not imply incompatibility, for a hat can be red and small at the same time.

4° Antonymy

Three subtypes of this relationship, which is also called «oppositeness», may be distinguished:

- complementarity: There is a relation of complementarity between two terms when the assertion of one term (e. g. *married* in *John is married*) implies the denial of the other (*single* in *John is single*). In fact the two terms completely divide a conceptual area between them, so that there is no in-between, no middle term («tertium non datur»).

Most complementaries are adjectives (E. *male :female*, *right :left*, F. *vivant :mort*, *vrai :faux*) or verbs (E. *to pass :to fail (an exam)*, F. *continuer :arrêter*). In the case of adjectives, a linguistic characteristic of complementary items is that they are not gradable: **John is more married*, F. **Le chien est très mort.*.

- polarity: The relation between the items in pairs like E. *big : small*, *young :old*, *beautiful :ugly*, *hot :cold*, etc. is one of polarity, and so is that between F. *facile :difficile*, *riche : pauvre*, *long :court*, etc. The principle of «tertium non datur» does not hold in this case, for *big* and *small*, *riche* and *pauvre* are in fact the extremes or poles of a scale, permitting intermediate positions. Therefore the assertion of one term does not entail the denial of the other: *not big* is not necessarily *small*, but may be *middle-sized*, and *pas riche* may be far from *pauvre*. Polar adjectives are therefore gradable: *bigger*, *older*, *most beautiful*, F. *plus facile*, *très riche*, etc.

The relative content of polar adjectives is also apparent from the fact that they are graded against different norms, depending on what is referred to: a small elephant is still a big animal, much bigger than a big mouse; bread is «old» after a few days, a dog after a few years, a man after many years.

Finally, it is also characteristic of polar adjectives that one of the two antonyms can be used in a neutral sense, i. e. without implying that the person or thing referred to possesses the quality denoted by the adjective. This term is called the «unmarked» term, and this neutral or unmarked use is typical in questions or statements about the degree of the gradable quality. Thus «How old is your brother?» and «My garden is only ten yards wide» do not imply that your brother is old or that my garden is wide; there is neutralization of the opposition in these cases.

- converseness or reciprocity: two terms are said to be converse when the relationship between the «things» referred to can be expressed from the point of view of either «thing». Thus *husband* and *wife*, *parent* and *child*, *buy* and *sell*, *above* and *below* (and their French equivalents) are in a relation of converseness or reciprocity because

if *John is Mary's husband*
then *Mary is John's wife*

if *George and Helen are Michael's parents*
then *Michael is George and Helen's child*

if *Fred sold a car to Henry*
then *Henry bought a car from Fred*

if *A major ranks above a captain*
then *A captain ranks below a major*

Converse terms imply each other; one term is like the mirror image of the other.

From a paradigmatic point of view the interrelations between items of the vocabulary form very complex networks. The word *father*, for example, is a synonym of *Dad*, a hyponym of *parent* and of *man*, a converse term of *son*, *daughter* and *child*, etc. On the other hand, this last item, apart from being a converse term of *father*, *mother* and *parent*, is a synonym of *offspring* and *progeny*, a superordinate term of *son* and *daughter*, etc.

II. 3.2. SYNTAGMATIC RELATIONS OF MEANING

Meaning relations not only exist between members of a paradigm, but can also be viewed from a sequential or syntagmatic point of view. What is examined then is how words relate to each other with regard to co-occurrence. It will then be found that some words do not combine into phrases because of selectional restrictions, i. e. because of their semantic content, as was illustrated in I. 7 above by such examples as **the dog smiles* and **to drink bread.* In other cases the unacceptable combination of words is simply due to idiosyncratic properties of the items concerned, i. e. to the preferential or exclusive company words keep, as in **to turn old* or **wide shoulders*, which will be rejected in favour of the collocations *to grow old* or *to get old,* and *broad shoulders.*

For a more extensive treatment of these phenomena see I. 7 above.

PART TWO

FRENCH-ENGLISH CONTRASTIVE LEXICOLOGY

INTRODUCTION

I. PURPOSE: Examining the limits of translational equivalence

Contrastive lexicology is the comparative study of the vocabularies of two or more languages. Its essential task is to examine how the data of human experience are reflected in the word material of the languages compared. Practically, the linguist will do this by examining whether and to what extent the words of one language can be said to be «translational equivalents» or «interlingual synonyms» of the words of another language.

«Translational equivalence» or «interlingual synonymy» is thus a central notion and needs some clarifying. For an item of language A to be fully equivalent to an item of language B, both must have identical communicative value in comparable linguistic contexts and in comparable situations, i. e. they must convey the same conceptual content, have the same connotations, belong to the same language variety, and enter into comparable collocations. Such «strict synonymy», which, as we have seen, is very rarely the case within one and the same language (i. e. intralingually), is not frequent either with words of different languages (i. e. interlingually).

The term «translational equivalence» is, however, often used in a weaker sense, i. e. the relation that holds between words which are regularly used as translations of each other and are presented as such in bilingual dictionaries. Thus the item *foot* is commonly considered as a translational equivalent of *pied*, even if *le pied d'une table* is rendered in English by *the leg of a table*. It is such «so-called translational equivalents» that we shall take as objects of our analysis in this survey. Our task then will be to discuss the different factors which account for the partial nature of the equivalence between French and English lexical items and, if possible, to make generalizations about them with regard to the general characteristics of the two lexical systems.

Let us illustrate equivalence and its limits with a few examples:

1. F. *thermostat*: E. *thermostat*: These technical terms may be said to be totally equivalent. In both languages this particular item is used to refer to a well-defined object. The same full equivalence may be found with words referring to internationally known items (F. *autoroute*: E. *motorway*, F. *aéroport*: E. *airport*, F. *cafétéria*: E. *cafeteria*) or sets of items (F. *lundi*, *mardi*, ...E. *Monday*, *Tuesday*, ...), and of course even in other categories of words.

2. F. *blessé*: E. *wounded*: These translation equivalents are only partial. There is a conceptual difference between the two items, in the sense that English makes a specific distinction between *wounded* (sustained in war or fighting), and another «equivalent» of *blessé*, viz. *injured* (as a result of an accident, for instance).

3. F. *échelle*: E. *ladder*: Here again, the equivalence is only partial, and again the difference is conceptual. Unlike the case described in 2, the divergence is not due here to a different organisation of the data of experience, but simply to the polysemous nature of one of the items, viz. of *échelle*, which is an equivalent of E. *ladder* in one of its meanings, but of *scale* in another one.

4. F. *gendarme*: E. -----. No translation equivalent is available in English, because the «thing meant» is totally absent in the world of experience of the English-speaking community.

5. F. *misogyne*: E. *woman-hater*: Partial equivalence from a connotative point of view, as the English item is more suggestive than the French one.

6. F. *commencer*: E. *to commence*: The equivalence is only partial for stylistic reasons, as the English item, unlike the French one, belongs to a formal register.

7. F. *large*: E. *wide*: Partial equivalence, because the use of *wide* (as its «synonym» *broad*) is subject to collocational constraints which do not apply to F. *large*.

Though the cases mentioned in 2 and 3 (and also in 4, for that matter) both illustrate conceptual divergence, it is important to see what distinguishes them. Example 2 is an illustration of the language-specificness of cognitive meaning, discussed at some length in I. 4. 10, whereby is meant that different languages may categorize the data of experience in different ways. In type 3 this is not the case, as the speakers of both languages here have both concepts, so that the difference is only a matter of diverging polysemy.

Example 4 represents cases of «cultural untranslatability», i. e. cases where the data of experience (the «realia») themselves are different in the speech communities concerned. What is meant is that even in closely related speech communities the extra-linguistic worlds of reality will differ in some respects: certain «things» (institutions, functions, activities, objects and other elements of culture) which are present in one community may be totally unknown or have only approximate correspondents in the other, which naturally leads to problems of translational equivalence. Thus what is denoted by F. *préfecture*, *baccalauréat*, *gendarme*, *carré blanc*, *béret*, or E. *public school*, *solicitor*, *coroner*, *bank holiday*, *haggis* is part of the experience of one speech community only. Dictionaries will in such cases resort to approximate counterparts or paraphrases, or simply borrow the foreign word.

2.METHOD: The problem of the «tertium comparationis»

Contrastive lexical analysis poses serious theoretical problems. As all comparison presupposes a «tertium comparationis», i.e. a standard outside the things compared, which may be used as a basis for comparison (in the way we use the yard or the mile to compare two distances), the question arises in contrastive lexicology what «tertium» can be used for the comparison of the semantic content of words.

As far as the conceptual aspect of word meaning is concerned, the only tertia available in the present state of linguistic knowledge would seem to be the distinctive semantic features revealed by componential analysis, in so far as they can be shown to be, if not universal, at least common to the languages compared.To discover these components, the analyst will have to rely on his own or informants' knowledge of both languages and cultures, on native speakers' reactions and on textual documentation (dictionaries, corpora).

The actual analytical technique may then consist in grouping semantically related words, i.e.in establishing corresponding semantic fields, and in listing the sets of features which distinguish the meanings of these words. A matching procedure on the basis of these «tertia» will then enable the analyst to establish equivalences and differences between the items of language A and language B. A rough analysis of the verbs of «pulling» («tirer») will illustrate this approach:

members of the field:

E.: *to pull* (superordinate term), *to drag*, *to haul*, *to trail*, *to tow*;
F.: *tirer* (superordinate term), *traîner*, *haler*, *remorquer*

list of distinctive features:

1 /subject: moving/
2 /object: vehicle/
3 /object: vessel/
4 /place: from river bank/
5 /direction: horizontal/
6 /direction: toward subject/
7 /manner: laborious/
8 /instrument: string or rope/

matching:

	drag	*haul*	*trail*	*tow*	*traîner*	*haler*	*remorquer*
1	+	±	+	+	+	+	+
2	-	-	-	+	-	-	+
3	-	±	-	+	-	+	+
4	-	±	-	±	-	+	-
5	+	±	+	+	+	+	+
6	-	±	-	-	-	-	-
7	+	+	-	+	+	+	+
8	-	±	+	+	-	+	+

The contrastive analysis shows that *traîner* is an equivalent of *to drag*, and potentially also of *to haul*; that *to tow* can be used as an equivalent of both *haler* and *remorquer*; that *to trail* has no real equivalent in that it is used with regard to light objects (*a child trailing a toy car*), which distinguishes this verb from *traîner*.

Of course, after all that was said in Part One, I.4.5 about the weaknesses of componential analysis, it will be clear that the technique just illustrated is of limited applicability. Apart from the fact that in many areas of the vocabulary oppositional features are vague and fuzzy, the very nature of the components raises a serious problem. As soon as they can no longer be seen as language-independent cognitive elements, they are simply words belonging to one of the vocabularies of the languages compared, which in turn raise the problem of equivalence. If we say, for instance, that the English lexical item *hero* and its «equivalent» in a distant oriental language both have a component /brave/, there will be real equivalence only if «bravery» has the same content in both speech communities (which is not necessarily the case: suicide, for example, may be seen as an act of courage in some cultures, and denote lack of courage in others). Such is the linguist's lot: language, which is his object of study, is at the same time his instrument.

With regard to the contrastive analysis of the connotative, stylistic and collocational meanings of interlingual « synonyms », the linguist will of course again have to start from empirical data (native informants, dictionaries, corpora), but little has been achieved in the way of systematic treatment of such data.

CHAPTER I: TRANSLATIONAL EQUIVALENCE IS ONLY PARTIAL

I.1. TRANSLATIONAL EQUIVALENCE IS ONLY PARTIAL FROM A CONCEPTUAL POINT OF VIEW

I.1.1. DIFFERENT ORGANISATION OF THE DATA OF EXPERIENCE

In this section we shall deal with cases of partial equivalence due to the language-specificness of conceptual meaning, i.e.to the fact that each language views and categorizes reality in its own, specific way (See Part One: I.4.10). Simplifying things a little, it can be said that such different organisation of the data of experience often implies one of two phenomena:

- one language further subdivides a semantic space or, to put it in componential terms, one language makes use of one or more distinctive features to make further conceptual distinctions within a semantic area. Thus the area covered by F.*blessé* corresponds to two sub-areas in English, covered respectively by *wounded* and *injured*. English here makes use of a distinctive feature which may be represented by /violence/, and which appears to be irrelevant in French.

- both languages cut up a semantic space in similar ways, but whereas one language has, in addition, a generic or superordinate term covering the whole area, the other language leaves the related meanings ungrouped. A case in point is F.*charcuterie*, which «groups» *jambon*, *saucisson*, etc.; English also has *ham*, *sausage*, etc., but no generic term to include all these items.

Subdividing is thus distinguished from grouping.

I.1.1.1.Further (and/or different) subdivision of a semantic space

Considering the difficulty of defining what exactly should be meant by the term «word» (See Part One, Introduction:II), only rough assessments can be made as to the number of words a given vocabulary contains. There can be no doubt, however, about the fact that the English word stock is considerably larger than the French one. According to Baquet (1974, 5), «le français, qui passe pour une langue précise, utilise moins de 100.000 mots pour traduire le volume des significations lexicales. L'anglais compte plus de 250.000 mots simples, auxquels s'ajoutent quelque 100.000 composés et dérivés. Loin derrière lui et le français viennent toutes les langues d'Europe, en particulier dans l'ordre : l'allemand, l'espagnol, l'italien». Baquet's figures seem to be on the low side, for both The Oxford English Dictionary and Webster's Third New International Dictionary, which are far from including all technical or regional items, list over half a million English words.

The quantitative superiority of English is due partly to the extraordinary easiness with which new words are created in this language through compounding, derivation or conversion, or simply coined on the basis of auditory or visual impressions. But it is also due to the liberal, «open-door» policy which the English language has always adopted with regard to foreign words. All through its history English has readily borrowed from the vocabularies of many other languages. Those that have made the most substantial contribution are French (especially from the Norman Conquest up to the end of the XIVth century, but of course also in modern times), Latin (at different periods, but especially during the XVIth century, at the time of the revival of classical learning), and Scandinavian (during the IXth, Xth and XIth centuries). According to Koziol's estimate only about one third of the English vocabulary is of Anglo-Saxon origin, whereas well over another third goes back to Norman French.

The presence of such a high percentage of words of foreign origin in the English vocabulary has its advantages and its disadvantages.With regard to the latter it has been pointed out that, as a result of borrowing, the specific resources of the native language have been weakened. Thus the process of compounding, characteristic of Old English and of Germanic languages in general, has lost some of its significance in Modern English (compare Dutch *hoop :wanhoop* and English *hope : despair*, Dutch *mens :menswaardig* and English *man :decent*). Also, and partially as a result of this, pairs or groups of words which are semantically connected no longer have any formal resemblance : *moon : lunar*, *sun : solar*, *nose : nasal*, *mouth : oral*, *house : domestic*, etc. But a great advantage no doubt outweighs these inconveniences : of the large number of new words only a minority were adopted to fill real gaps in the English vocabulary; the large majority were used as near-synonyms of already existing words, enabling the language user to express delicate and subtle nuances of meaning which could not be rendered before and often cannot be rendered in other languages. This existence of large groups of near-synonymous words in English (e.g.*male*, *manly*, *mannish*, *manlike*, *masculine*, *virile*, or *brave*, *courageous*, *unafraid*, *fearless*, *intrepid*, *valiant*, *valorous*, *dauntless*, *undaunted*, *doughty*, *bold*, *audacious*) may be a problem for the foreign learner, but provides the one who has mastered such a vocabulary with great possibilities for conceptually precise and stylistically appropriate expression.

The English vocabulary thus tends to be more concrete and precise, richer in expressive details, whereas the French vocabulary is more generic and abstract. « L'esprit anglais, qui tient à une certaine objectivité à l'égard des faits et choses du réel, se contente de les montrer dans leur aspect extérieur, d'en saisir les détails concrets, perceptibles, tangibles, contrôlables par tous ». As to the « esprit français », « moins que le dehors, c'est le dedans des choses, leur pourquoi et leur comment qui l'intéressent. Négligeant le détail, il dégage plutôt les grandes lignes, le résultat final. Aussi les mots qu'il emploie revêtent-ils un caractère d'abstraction plus poussé qu'en anglais » (Van Hoof, 1989, 49). Examples often mentioned are F.*être* (in the sense of « se trouver »), where English of course has *to be*, but frequently prefers to be more specific by using *to stand*, *to lie* or *to hang* (*the piano stood in the corner*, *the book was lying on the table*, *the portrait hangs on the wall*), or F.*aller*, where English has *to go*, but will often prefer *to walk*, *to drive*, *to ride* etc., according to the precise activity denoted.

To illustrate this further, let us start with a number of relatively simple cases where a semantic space, covered by one lexical item in French, is split up in English:

affiche	*poster* *bill*
anniversaire	*anniversary* *birthday*
archives	*archives* *records*
assassiner	*to murder* *to assassinate*
blessé	*injured* *wounded*
bois	*wood* *timber* *lumber*
bouquet	*bouquet* *bunch* *posy*

brin	*blade* *sprig* *twig* *wisp*
camion	*lorry* *van*
carte (geogr.)	*map* *chart*
chaque	*every* *each* *either*
cimetière	*cemetery* *churchyard*
coiffeur	*hairdresser* *barber*
confiture	*jam* *marmalade*
fermer	*to close* *to shut* *to lock*
jeu	*game* *play*
louer	*to hire* *to rent*
marque	*trademark* *brand* *make*
panier	*basket* *hamper*
président	*president* *chairman*
promenade	*walk, stroll* *drive* *ride* *sail*

réparer	*to repair* *to mend*
rougir	*to flush* *to blush*
singe	*monkey* *ape*
traîneau	*sleigh* *sledge*
tache	*spot* *stain* *blot* *smudge* *speck*
troupeau	*herd* *flock* *pride* *gaggle*
usine	*factory* *works* *mill*
voyage	*journey* *trip* *voyage* *travel (- agency, - sickness)*

In many other cases the semantic space is covered by several lexemes in both languages, but reflects more expressive detail in English. This is particularly striking in the vocabulary of sensory perception, as the first few examples show. (The lists of items are not necessarily exhaustive; words which are very rarely used have been omitted).

F. *odeur, senteur, parfum, puanteur, relent*
E. *smell, odour, scent, fragrance, perfume, stink, stench, reek*

F. *briller, (re)luire, étinceler, scintiller, rutiler, chatoyer, rougeoyer, pétiller, clignoter*
E. *shine, blaze, twinkle, sparkle, glint, glow, gleam, glance, glimmer, glitter, glisten, glare, flash, flicker*

F. *mouillé, trempé, humide, moite*

E. *wet, soaked, drenched, humid, damp, dank, clammy, muggy, moist*

F. *crier, hurler, brailler, gueuler*
E. *shout, scream, screech, squeal, shriek, yell, howl, roar, cry*

F. *regarder, dévisager, se renfrogner*
E. *look, glance, gaze, stare, frown, scold*

F. *frapper, battre, rosser, gifler, fustiger, fouetter, flageller*
E. *hit, strike, knock, beat, thrash, slap, smack, spank, cane, whip, flog*

F. *rire, sourire, glousser, ricaner, s'esclaffer, pouffer*
E. *laugh, smile, chuckle, giggle, grin, smirk, leer, snigger, guffaw*

F. *bord, bordure, rive, rivage, lisière, orée, tranche, ourlet*
E. *edge, bank, shore, brim, brink, rim, hem, kerb*

F. *brume, brouillard*
E. *haze, mist, fog, smog*

F. *client, patient, pensionnaire*
E. *customer, client, patient, patron, fare, visitor, guest*

F. *couper, hacher, tailler, rogner, trancher*
E. *cut, carve, chop, clip, trim, snip, mince, slit, slice*

F. *mousse, écume*
E. *foam, froth, suds, lather, scum*

F. *glisser, déraper*
E. *slide, glide, slip, skid*

F. *marcher, cheminer, arpenter, trotter, trottiner*
E. *walk, march, stride, stalk, pace, plod, trudge, toddle*

F. *prendre, saisir, attraper, empoigner*
E. *take, seize, catch, grab, snatch, grasp, grip*

F. *tirer, traîner, remorquer, haler, tirailler*
E. *pull, draw, drag, trail, tow, tug, jerk, haul*

It is worth pointing out here too, even if it is not strictly within the scope of this paragraph 1.1.1.1, that English, due to the easiness with which it creates new words by combining existing items into compounds, by deriving words from each other and by converting words from one class to another, may express new meanings which are not lexicalized in the French language, where they can only be rendered by means of paraphrases.

compounds:

(this house is)*childproof* : F.(cette maison est) sans danger pour les enfants
camera-shy (people) : (des gens) qui n'aiment pas être photographiés
to house-sit (for sb) : garder la maison (pour qqn)
(women) *outnumber* (men) : (les femmes) sont plus nombreuses que (les hommes)
quick-assembly (furniture) : (meubles) à monter soi-même
boy-meets-girl stories : (histoires) romantiques conventionnelles

By adding adverbial particles to existing verbs, English creates phrasal verbs, where French again often lacks semantically equivalent lexical items.This type of compounding is extremely productive:

to stop : *s'arrêter*
to stop by : s'arrêter en passant
to stop up : ne pas se coucher, rester debout
to stop off : faire une courte halte
to stop over : faire une halte

to think : *penser*
to think back : essayer de se souvenir
to think out : réfléchir à fond
to think through : examiner en détail
to think up : avoir l'idée de, inventer

derivations: By means of suffixation with e.g.*-dom*, *-hood*, *-ness* or -*ship* English enriches its vocabulary with words denoting abstract notions not always lexicalized in French:

dukedom : titre de duc
heathendom : le monde païen
professordom : le milieu des professeurs

bachelorhood : condition de vieux garçon
spinsterhood : condition de vieille fille
orphanhood : condition d'orphelin

recentness : nature récente
out-of-dateness: caractère suranné, vieilli
sinfulness: caractère coupable

leadership : sens du commandement
authorship : paternité littéraire, métier d'écrivain
statesmanship : habileté politique, diplomatie

Another productive device is the use of the suffix *-ly* to derive adverbs from participles or adjectives, where French has no corresponding adverbial lexeme:

admittedly : de l'aveu général, il faut le reconnaître
allegedly : à ce que l'on prétend, paraît-il
deservedly : à juste titre
knowingly : en connaissance de cause, d'un air entendu
reproachfully : d'un air de reproche
reluctantly : à contre-coeur, à son corps défendant

conversion: This word formation process, whereby an item is transferred to another word class without the addition of a suffix, is remarkably productive in English. It also contributes to the constant enrichment of the vocabulary in areas where French may have a lexical gap.This is frequently the case with denominal verbs such as

to tunnel : creuser un tunnel, *to elbow* (through sth): se frayer un passage à travers (en jouant des coudes), *to hoover* : passer à l'aspirateur, *to treasure* : garder préciseusement, *to veto* : opposer son veto, *to helicopter* : transporter en hélicoptère.

Instances of the opposite phenomenon, i.e. where the English vocabulary is vaguer than the French one, are of course not infrequent. Zajicek (1965, 7) even claims that the French vocabulary is on the whole more precise in cases of concrete reference. This is probably going a bit far, but he observes quite rightly that « Ainsi, dans le cas des vocables élémentaires, on s'aperçoit à l'usage que *book* n'est pas exactement *livre*, en ce sens que le mot français suggère l'idée de lecture, tandis que son équivalent habituel en anglais ne connaît pas semblable restriction (+ *cahier*, *registre*, *carnet*...). *Maison* désigne une habitation réservée exclusivement à l'homme ou à sa représentation, tandis que *house* étend sa signification bien au-delà de cette notion (*cow-house*, *hen-house*, *ape-house*, *light-house*, etc.) ». The following are a few other cases where French makes distinctions not used in English:

E.	*bell*	F.	*cloche*, *clochette* *grelot* *sonnette*

ball	*balle* *ballon* *boule* (billard, croquet) *bille* (billard)
bone	*os* *arête*
box	*boîte* *caisse* *coffret*
break	*casser* *briser* *rompre*
brush	*brosse* *balai* *pinceau*
hook	*crochet* *patère* *agrafe* *hameçon*
candle	*bougie* *chandelle* *cierge*
climb	*monter* *grimper* *escalader*
hair	*cheveu* *poil*
end	*fin* *bout* *extrémité*
handle	*anse* *manche* *poignée* *bras* (pompe) *manivelle*
river	*fleuve* *rivière*

sharpen	*aiguiser* *tailler*
shell	*coquille* *coquillage* *carapace* *cosse*
size	*grandeur* *dimension* *volume* *taille* *format* *pointure*
word	*mot* *parole*

While it was observed above that English has a greater variety of suffixes (*-dom*, *-hood*, *-ness*, *-ship*) for abstract derivation, French is perhaps somewhat richer in morphological means to distinguish concrete reference:

bell	*cloche* *clochette*
plank	*planche* *planchette*
door	*porte* *portière*
rock	*roc* *roche* *rocher*
wall	*mur* *muret* *muraille*

It is true that English may in some cases further specify the comparatively vague meanings just discussed, viz. by using compound forms (*arête* : *fishbone*, *hameçon* : *fish-hook*, *portière* : *car-door*). But this is mainly done when the meanings are not clear from the context.

I.1.1.2. Grouping a number of subfields by means of a generic term

While in all the cases described so far one of the two languages is more specific than the other, in other cases English and French make comparable distinctions, but only one of both languages has, in addition to the specific items, a general or superordinate term to embrace them all.

A few examples are:

	F.		E.	
	frère		brother	*sibling*
	soeur		sister	
	noix		walnut	*nuts*
	noisette		hazelnut	
	amande		almond	
	etc.		etc.	
	prix		prize	*award*
	bourse d'études		scholarship	
	subvention		grant	
	distinction honorifique		honorary dist.	
charcuterie	jambon		ham	
	saucisson		sausage	
	etc.		etc.	
deux-roues	bicyclette		bicycle	
	vélomoteur		moped	
	motocyclette		motorcycle	
boissons	lait	*beverage*	milk	*drinks*
	café		coffee	
	thé		tea	
	vin		wine	
	bière		beer	
	eau		water	
	whisky		whisky	
	sherry		sherry	
	etc.		etc.	

artiste	peintre	painter	*artist*
	sculpteur	sculptor	*artist*
	musicien	musician	*artist*
	acteur	actor	*artiste*
	chanteur	singer	*artiste*
	danseur	dancer	*artiste*
	fantaisiste	entertainer	*artiste*
spectacle	théâtre	theatre	*entertainment*
	opéra	opera	*entertainment*
	ballet	ballet	*entertainment*
	concert	concert	*entertainment*
	cinéma	cinema	*entertainment*
	music hall	music hall	*entertainment*
	variétés	show	*entertainment*
	cirque	circus	*entertainment*
	expositions	exhibitions	*entertainment*
	visites	visits	*entertainment*
	promenades (guidées)	walks	*entertainment*

I.1.2. FURTHER OR DIFFERENT EXTENSION OF MEANING (DIVERGING POLYSEMY)

As was pointed out in I.9, practically all vocabulary items have extended their original meaning and are therefore polysemous. But this polysemy may of course diverge from one language to another, in the sense that a word in language A and a word in language B may have one (or more) meaning(s) in common, but may have further extended this (these) common meaning(s) in different, specific ways, so that the translational equivalence is only partial.

It is important to see the difference between the phenomenon referred to here and the one just dealt with in I.1.1. In the latter case what was felt as a global conceptual meaning in one language was further differentiated in the other, so that we could speak of a different organisation of reality (F.*blessé* : E.*wounded*, *injured*). In the cases dealt with here both languages distinguish the same meanings, but whereas one language expresses them by one and the same, polysemous item (F.*échelle*), the other makes use of two different items (E.*ladder*, *scale*). It is of course true that the distinction between these two types of cases is not always easy to make, as it may be difficult to decide whether the total conceptual meaning of a word ought to be seen as « global » or not (cfr.I.9). The difference between the two phenomena may be represented as follows:

blessé	wounded
	injured

échelle 1	ladder
échelle 2	scale

In closely related languages there are of course cases where the extension of meaning is partially or even wholly parallel. F.*homme*, E.*man* and F.*langue*, E.*tongue* are cases in point:

F.*homme*	1.human being 2.male human being	E.*man*
F.*langue*	1.organ of speech 2.communication system	E.*tongue*

As a rule, however, one or more of the secondary meanings are either missing in the «equivalent», or do not coincide.Two different types of relationships may therefore hold between translational equivalents with diverging polysemy: inclusion and overlap.

E.*learn* and F.*apprendre* represent a case of inclusion, as the English item has fewer senses than the French one and as they are all included in the latter:

E.*learn* F.*apprendre*

1. to gain knowledge or acquire skill
   acquérir une connaissance, une aptitude

2. to become informed of something
   être informé de quelque chose

F.*apprendre*

3. enseigner (=E.*to teach*)

4. annoncer (=E.*to tell, to announce*)

E.*leaf* and F.*feuille*, on the other hand, are an instance of overlap: they share a number of senses, but have specific ones in addition :

E.*leaf* F.*feuille*

1. main organ of photosynthesis in plants
   partie des végétaux qui...

2. sheet of paper in a book
   un des éléments en papier qui composent un livre

E.*leaf*

3. hinged or sliding extension to a table
   (=F.*rabat*, *abattant*, *rallonge*)

F.*feuille*

3. plaque mince d'une matière quelconque
   (=E.*sheet*)

Erroneous meaning extension by analogy with the «equivalent» in the first language is an extremely frequent phenomenon in the process of foreign language acquisition. Thus errors of the type **he learnt me how to swim*, **the foot of the table* or **I assisted at the meeting* are very common in the English of French speaking learners (especially if the items concerned are «faux amis», i.e.when they resemble each other formally, as in the last example.See Chapter II). The following is only a very small sample of cases where a polysemous French item corresponds to two or more distinct words in English. On the whole it would seem that the opposite is somewhat less often the case.

ancien	*ancient* (the ancient authors, the ancients) *former*, *previous* (my former teacher) *old* (the old boys/girls, the former pupils, the alumni) *antique* (antique furniture)
apprécier	*to appreciate* (a good thing) *to estimate*, *to assess*, *to appraise*
apprendre	*to learn* (English) *to teach* (someone English) *to tell*(the news to everybody)
assister	*to assist* (an old lady) *to attend* (a meeting)

assistance	*assistance, help, aid* *audience*
assurer	*to assure* (I can assure you that...) *to insure* (one's car) *to ensure, to guarantee* (prompt delivery)
base	*base* (of a statue, a triangle=lower part; naval base, military base) *basis* (his arguments have a sound basis)
bouton	*button* (of a dress, a coat) *(push-)button* (of a bell) *knob* (of a radio) *bud* (the trees are in bud) *spot, pimple* (on the face)
bras	*arm* (of a person, of a chair, of the sea) *branch* (of a river) *handle* (of a pump)
canal	*canal* (the Suez canal) *channel* (abstract: TV channel)
cheminée	*chimney* (on the roof), *funnel* (of a ship) *fireplace, hearth* *mantelpiece* (frame above and at the sides of a fireplace)
choeur	*choir* (group of people trained to sing together) *chorus* (group of people who recite, sing or dance in a play)
ciel	*sky* *heaven*
conscience	*conscience* (to do something for conscience' sake) *consciousness* (to act in full consciousness) *conscientiousness* (to act with conscientiousness)
contrôler	*to inspect, to check* (documents, luggage) *to control, to dominate* (a country, an aircraft, oneself)
couronne	*crown* (the royal crown) *wreath* (of flowers)
creuser	*to dig* (the garden) *to delve* (into a person's past)

découvrir	*to discover* (Columbus discovered America) *to uncover* (the patient uncovered himself)
défendre	*to defend* (one's country, one's rights) *to prohibit* (smoking in an office)
défense	*defence* (the defence of the oppressed) *prohibition*(défense de fumer:no smoking) *tusk* (of an elephant)
*dent*t	*tooth* *prong* (of a fork) *cog* (of a wheel
disque	*disc* (the disc of the full moon) *discus* (the record in discus-throwing) *record* (a long-playing record)
dos	*back* (of a person, a seat, an envelope) *spine* (of a book)
doubler	*to double* (a person's salary) *to dub* (the sound track of a film) *to overtake* (a car on the road)
doux	*soft*, *smooth* (touch) *sweet* (taste, perfume, memory) *mild* (climate, weather) *gentle* (person, manners, character)
échelle	*ladder* (he fell off the ladder) *scale* (a map on a scale of l cm to 5 km)
échouer	*to fail* (in an exam, in an attempt) *to be stranded, to be grounded*(of a ship)
économie	*economics* (science) *economy* (l.operation of a country's money supply, industry and trade; 2.careful use of money, time, effort, etc.)
économique	*economic* (economic geography) *economical* (an economical car)
ennui	*trouble* *boredom*
envie	*desire*, *longing* (avoir envie:to feel like) *envy*, *jealousy*

étranger	*stranger* (person one does not know) *foreigner* (person from a country other than one's own) *alien* (person who is not a naturalized citizen of the country he or she is living in)
expérience	*experience* (he is too young and has no experience; tell me about your experiences as a pilot) *experiment* (to carry out experiments in a laboratory)
femme	*woman* *wife*
fleur	*flower* *blossom*, *bloom* (the trees are in blossom; the roses are in bloom)
gagner	*to win* (a prize, a race) *to earn* (money, one's living) *to gain* (time, ground=to increase, to add)
garçon	*boy* *waiter*
historique	*historic* (a historic event = important in history, famous) *historical* (a historical novel, h.research = connected with history as a study)
isoler	*isolate* (a word in a context, an event) *insulate* (=to prevent the transmission of electricity, heat or sound by means of a non-conducting material)
ivresse	*drunkenness*, *intoxication* (alcohol) *rapture*, *intoxication* (delight)
humain	*human* (related to man: human nature) *humane* (showing human kindness: a humane judge, a humane act)
maigre	*thin*, *lean*, *skinny*, *slim* (lacking in flesh) *meagre*, *scanty* (small in quantity and quality:a meagre meal, meagre response)
manifestation	*expression* (of feelings, opinions) *appearance* (of a disease) *demonstration* (political)
neutre	*neutral* *neuter* (grammar)

nu	*naked*, *nude* (naked bodies= without clothes) *bare* (bare head, feet, hands = without covering or protection)
occasion	*occasion*, *time*, *occurrence* (on the occasion of his birthday, on several occasions) *occasion*, *cause* (to give occasion for scandal, there is no occasion to be alarmed) *opportunity*, *chance* (I had the opportunity to meet him) *bargain* (That's a bargain!) *second-hand* (a second-hand car)
ombre	*shadow* (projected by a person, a tree, etc.) *shade* (as opposed to a sunlit area)
oriental	*oriental* (of the Orient: oriental art) *eastern* (of the East: Eastern Europe)
parents	*parents* (father and mother) *relatives*, *relations* (uncle, aunt, etc.)
pièce	*piece*(to fall to pieces) *room* (the adjoining room) *play* (a play in three acts) *document* (an important document)
pied	*foot* (of a person, a mountain, a wall) *leg* (of a table) *stem* (of a glass) *head* (of celery)
porter	*to carry* (bags, a suitcase) *to wear* (clothes, glasses, a hat, lipstick) *to bear* (the marks of a blow = to show) (a name = to be known by)
prix	*price* (of goods), *fee* (for tuition, an examination, membership, professional services of a doctor, etc.), *fare* (for a journey by bus, taxi, etc.) *prize* (award)
profond	*deep* (river, sympathy) *profound* (sympathy)
richesse	*riches* (all his riches are no good to him) *richness* (the richness of the colours)

retraite	*retreat* (strategic, religious) *retirement* (the age of retirement)
séminaire	*seminary* (for future priests) *seminar* (discussion group)
terre	*earth* (planet: the moon goes round the earth) *world* (the earth with all its inhabitants: the richest man in the world) *ground* (surface of the earth: don't lie on the ground) *land* (as opposed to sea: to travel over land, to sight land)
verre	*glass* (I broke my glass) *drink* (He bought me a drink)
voix	*voice* (to raise one's voice) *vote* (to put sth to the vote)

In this long list no reference has been made to the causes of the polysemy of the French items. Metonymic extension of meaning seems to be at work more often in this language than in English, where the use of different items is frequently preferred. In fact a great variety of subtypes might be distinguished, but only a few illustrations are given here:

1° the name of a substance is given to the object made of it:

argent	*silver* *money*	*pain*	*bread* *loaf of bread*
carton	*cardboard* *cardboard box*	*papier*	*paper* *sheet of paper*
fer	*iron* *iron bar*	*savon*	*soap* *bar of soap*

2° the name of an activity, a technique, a business or industry is given to the place where the activity etc. occurs and/or to the product or object of the activity etc.

banque	*banking* *bank*
bâtiment	*building trade* *building*

cuisine	*cooking* *kitchen* *food*
épicerie	*grocery* *grocer's* *groceries*
imprimerie	*printing* *printing house/works*
lingerie	*linen trade* *linen closet* *lingerie, underwear*
quincaillerie	*hardware trade* *hardware store* *hardware*

3° the name of an animal is used for its meat:

boeuf	*bullock, ox* *beef*	*porc*	*pig* *pork*
mouton	*sheep* *mutton*	*veau*	*calf* *veal*

4° the name of a room is used for the furniture in it:

chambre à coucher	*bedroom* *suite of bedroom furniture*
salon	*living room* *living room suite*
bureau	*study, office* *writing-table, desk*

5° the name of an instrument is used for the person playing it:

clairon	*bugle* *bugler*	*tambour*	*drum* *drummer*

6° the name of the container is used for the contents:

assiette	*plate* *plateful*	*sceau*	*pail* *pailful*

Another frequent case of polysemy due to metonymy can be observed in the abstract vocabulary of French, when one and the same word is used 1° to denote an action or process, and 2° to denote a particular instance of this action or process or what results from it. English as a rule has separate items (with the verbal noun in *-ing*, in addition to the infinitive (which is also available in French) often denoting the action or process), so that the lexical richness of English again emerges at this abstract level. Examples are:

don	*giving* *gift*	*jeu*	*playing* *play*
échappée	*escaping* *escape*	*rouille*	*rusting* *rust*
émeute	*rioting* *riot*	*signature*	*signing* *signature*
pari	*betting* *bet*	*traduction*	*translating* *translation*

There are of course also innumerable cases where the polysemy of the English item may lead the French learner astray. Thus, in the decoding process, a French speaker who is unaware of the polysemous nature of *argument* or *anxious*, may fail to interpret correctly such sentences as *The argument made her cry* or *He is anxious to see you.* But problems of decoding are on the whole less critical, as context and situation often preclude misunderstanding or at least make it less likely. We can therefore limit ourselves to giving a small selection of potential problem words in English: *address*, *anxious*, *appear*, *apply*, *argument*, *audience*, *bone*, *character*, *confidence*, *country*, *disgrace*, *evidence*, *figure*, *gallant*, *gentleman*, *introduce*, *medicine*, *obtain*, *occupation*, *particular*, *pity*, *plain*, *positive*, *replace*, *return*, *scandal*, *sentence*, *spirits*, *succeed*, *to wonder*.

I.2. TRANSLATIONAL EQUIVALENCE IS ONLY PARTIAL FROM A CONNOTATIVE POINT OF VIEW

The connotation of a word is what the word conveys, conceptually or emotionally, in addition to its essential, distinctive meaning content. This may of course vary, for one and the same language, from one period to another, from one area to another and even from one speaker or group of speakers to another.

It was pointed out in I.5 of Part One that connotations may find their origin 1°in the phonetic or morphological form of words, 2°in the characteristics of the referent, 3°in the secondary meaning of words, which may «rub off» on their basic meaning.

If, from a contrastive point of view, we first look at phonetic form, it is only natural that onomatopeias, which are based on direct phonic imitation, should often be in close one-to-one correspondence (E.*cuckoo* : F.*coucou*; E.*cackle* : F.*caqueter*; E.*crack* : F.*craquer*, etc.). But even when the phonetic structure of words is not an acoustic echo of what it refers to but merely a case of phonetic symbolism, i.e. produces some sensory or psychic effect, English and French are to some extent parallel. Thus, as was pointed out in I.1, in both languages the initial consonants *fl-* are suggestive of lightness and fluidity (E.*fly*, *flutter*, *flow*, *flee*, *flit*, etc., F.*flots*, *flotter*, *fluide*, *fleuve*, *flute*, etc.), the vowel *i* frequently suggests smallness (E.*tip*, *pip*, *sip*, *mini-*, *tiny*, *little*, etc., F.*petit*, *mignon*, *minime*, *subtil*, etc.), and gemination produces various psychological effects (E.*chitchat*, *flip-flop*, *jingle-jangle*, etc., F.*et patati et patata*, *cahin-caha*, *clopin-clopant*, etc.). But the relationship between sounds and their effects is of course also partially language-specific, so that the parallelism cannot be pushed too far. One important difference between the two languages is that English seems to make wider use of phonetic symbolism. It has developed or created large numbers of suggestive (mostly monosyllabic) onomatopeias such as the sound-imitating verbs *to bang*, *to boom*, *to buzz*, *to clash*, *to clatter*, *to click*, *to crack*, *to hiss*, *to honk*, *to hum*, *to lash*, *to purr*, *to slam*, *to splash*, *to snap*, *to tap*, *to whirr*, *to whiz* etc., for many of which French lacks a lexical equivalent.

As far as the morphological structure of words is concerned, the processes of derivation and compounding, which are so productive in English, have enriched this language with many verbs, nouns and adjectives which convey a concrete, descriptive and suggestive connotation, often to be rendered in French by a more abstract and static item or by a paraphrase. Consider such prefixed verbs as

E.	F.
to unblock (a road)	*dégager* (une route)
to undo (sb's work)	*détruire* (l'oeuvre de qqn)
to unburden (one's conscience)	*soulager* (sa conscience)
to unlatch (a door)	*enlever* (le loquet)
to unnerve (a person)	*faire perdre courage*(à qqn)
unquote (=imperative)	*«fin de citation»*
to unseat (an MP)	*faire perdre son siège* (à un député)
to unveil (a statue)	*inaugurer* (une statue)
to upgrade (an employee)	*promouvoir* (un employé)
to update (a report)	*mettre à jour* (un rapport)
to uproot (a person from his home)	*arracher* (qqn à son foyer)

Consider also English phrasal and prepositional verbs. Many actions or events can be expressed in English either by a simple verb (*to reject* a proposal) or by a phrasal or prepositional verb (*to brush aside* a proposal). By using the latter form, which is especially characteristic of informal style, English again marks its preference for a concrete and suggestive, often even «photographic» or kinetic representation of things, where the French equivalent will again be more abstract and static. Compare:

E. *to put across* (a message)	F. *communiquer* (un message)
to brush aside (a proposal)	*écarter* (une proposition)
to do away with (a law)	*abolir* (une loi)
to keep away from (drink)	*s'abstenir de* (boire)
to back down	*se dérober, se dégonfler*
to lay down (a rule)	*établir* (une règle)
to look down on (a person)	*mépriser* (une personne)
to cut down on (expenses)	*réduire* (les dépenses)
to play down (a difference)	*minimiser* (une différence)
to stand down	*démissionner, se désister*
to look forward to (a party)	*attendre avec impatience*
to put forward (an opinion)	*exprimer une opinion*
to break in on (a conversation)	*interrompre*
to fall in	*s'effondrer*
to go into (a matter)	*examiner* (une question)
to talk sb into doing sth	*persuader* (qqn de faire qqch)
to talk sb out of doing sth	*dissuader* (qqn de faire qqch)
to run into sb	*rencontrer qqn par hasard*
to break off (relations)	*rompre* (les relations)
to call off (an appointment)	*annuler* (un rendez-vous)
to put off (a meeting)	*remettre à plus tard*
to turn off (the light)	*éteindre* (la lumière)
to put on (airs)	*se donner* (des airs)
to sign on (as a ship's boy)	*se faire engager* (comme mousse)
to run out of (money)	*manquer d'* (argent)
to turn out (all right)	(bien) *finir*
to walk out on (a partner)	*plaquer* (un partenaire)
to back up (a candidate)	*soutenir* (un candidat)
to come up with (an idea)	*proposer* (une idée)
to cut up (meat)	*découper* (la viande)
to look up to (a person)	*avoir du respect pour* (qqn)
to make up (a story)	*inventer* (une histoire)
to show up	*être visible, manifeste*
to split up (the work)	*partager, répartir*
to ring up (a friend)	*téléphoner à* (un ami)
to stand up for (a principle)	*défendre* (un principe)

English is also remarkably rich in motivated, expressive noun and adjective compounds, often corresponding to more or less opaque lexical items in French. A few examples are:

E.	*armchair*	F.	*fauteuil*
	armhole		*entournure*
	bookkeeper		*comptable*
	bullfighter		*toréador*
	dress rehearsal		*répétition générale*
	eyelids		*paupières*
	firefly		*luciole*
	housekeeper		*concierge*
	grass snake		*couleuvre*
	seal-ring		*chevalière*
	shipowner		*armateur*
	sleepwalker		*somnambule*
	violin maker		*luthier*
	watercolour		*aquarelle*
	water-sprinkler		*goupillon*
	woman hater		*misogyne*

E.	*absent-minded*	F.	*distrait*
	close-mouthed		*taciturne*
	four-legged		*quadrupède*
	long-sighted		*presbyte*
	short-sighted		*myope*
	short-lived		*éphémère*
	small-minded		*mesquin*
	twin-bladed		*bipale*
	Y-shaped		*sous forme d'Y*

Finally, the great facility with which words shift from one class to another (or: undergo « zero conversion ») in English also contributes to more suggestive expression. This is the case, for example, with the deverbal nouns in phrases such as

E.	*on the move*	F.	*en mouvement .*
	on the run		*en cavale*
	to give sth a pull/a push		*tirer (sur)/pousser*
	his speech *hadn't much bite*		son discours *manquait de mordant*
	there's no give in this cloth		ce tissu *ne prête pas*
	these are *our own make*		ceux-ci sont *fabriqués par nous*
	the feel of wool		*la sensation* de laine
	the look of him		*son allure*

It is these connotations of concreteness, suggestiveness and dynamism, coupled with the more differentiated conceptualisation described in I.1 above, which have led French linguists to admit that « L'anglais voit les choses volontiers par le dehors, le français par le dedans. L'anglais grâce à ses particules et ses verbes concrets montre les mouvements, dessine les contours des choses et des êtres, plus que ne le fait le français » (Bonnerot et al., 1963, 2). Quite a long time ago the French literary critic Taine observed that « Traduire en français une phrase anglaise, c'est copier au crayon gris une figure en couleur. Réduisant ainsi les aspects et les qualités des choses, l'esprit français aboutit à des idées générales, c'est-à-dire simples, qu'il aligne dans un ordre simplifié, celui de la logique » (quoted by A.Chevrillon, RDM, 1908).

The connotation of a word may have to do with the (non-distinctive) characteristics of its referent. In closely related languages referents frequently have the same or similar characteristics, so that the words to denote them will have comparable connotations. This holds true, for instance, for the pairs *mother* and *mère*, *home* and *chez soi*, *immigrant* and *immigré*, and the taboo words discussed in Part One, I.5. In many other cases, however, the connotative meanings of conceptual equivalents may, for cultural reasons, be different. Thus *queen* and *tea* on the whole probably have a more favourable connotation than *reine* and *thé*, given the English people's affection for their sovereign and their unquenchable thirst for tea, and the Frenchman's received image of Marie-Antoinette and his predilection for coffee.

More or less the same thing may be said in connection with the third factor to which connotative meanings may be ascribed: the secondary meaning of a word. To the extent that translational equivalents have parallel extensions of meaning, their connotations may coincide: the examples given in I.5 of Part One, *peasant* and *paysan*, *gay* and *gai*, *intercourse* and *rapports*, as also *drug* and *drogue* (with their secondary meanings of, respectively, « unmannered person », « homosexual », « sexual intercourse », « narcotic drug ») are cases in point. Their use in the basic sense is sometimes avoided because of the unfavourable connotation springing from the secondary sense. Of course, more often than not basic translation equivalents show diverging polysemy, in which case there may be a given connotation in one language but not in the other.Thus F.*jeune fille* is often preferred to *fille* because of the occasional use of the latter item in the sense of *prostitute*, but E.*girl* does not raise such a problem.Thus also, in English *back of* may sometimes be preferred to the preposition *behind* (*back of the house*), because the latter item, when used as a noun, denotes « the part of the body on which one sits ».

I.3. TRANSLATIONAL EQUIVALENCE IS ONLY PARTIAL FROM A STYLISTIC POINT OF VIEW

In I.1.1.1 above it was pointed out that English has enriched its vocabulary mainly by borrowing words from a considerable number of languages, and that this has resulted in the existence of a wealth of near-synonyms enabling the English speaker or writer to make more delicate and subtle distinctions on the level of conceptual meaning than is possible in many other languages.

The borrowing of Latin and Greek words, but especially of French words, has also had an important effect on the English language from a stylistic point of view.

The earliest Latin and Greek elements (e.g.*wine*, *street*, *wall*, *inch*; *church*, *angel*, *devil*, *bishop* -the latter group via Latin, like almost all Greek words) were imported into English from 450 onwards by the Anglo-Saxon invaders, who had adopted many Latin words on the continent, and by the Roman missionaries from 597 onwards. But it is the revival of classical learning in the XVIth century that led to the adoption of large numbers of Latin and Greek words. Ever since, the presence of such words has been a characteristic of learned and scientific style in English as in many other languages. Of the thousands of specialized terms *deficit*, *alibi*, *memento*, *radium*, *spectrum*, all of Latin origin, and *psychology*, *pediatrics*, *chronology*, *atomic*, *isotope*, *proton*, etc. , all of Greek origin, are only a few examples.

French was introduced into England at the time of the Norman Conquest (1066) and for more than two centuries gradually interpenetrated the native language far more deeply than Latin or Greek had ever done. The social conditions of this change, i.e.the fact that French was the language spoken by the invading noblemen and used to make laws, to rule the Church and to dispense teaching gave it much prestige and has had permanent consequences with regard to style in English. Though it can of course not be claimed that the Romance component of the English vocabulary is as a whole stylistically more elevated than the Anglo-Saxon one (for *cry*, *face*, *fool*, *pity*, *river*, *rock*, *table*, *uncle* etc. etc. are quite everyday words in present-day English), it is nevertheless true that words of French origin are as a rule more intellectual, abstract or formal than their Germanic «synonyms». Zajicek (1965, 12) speaks of a «lexique anglais à double clavier», and Baugh (1957, 225) of «synonyms at three levels»: Latin, French and native, corresponding to «learned», «literary» and «popular» style, as illustrated by *to ascend*, *to mount*, *to rise*; *to interrogate*, *to question*, *to ask*; *probity*, *virtue*, *goodness*; (though the differences between these items are clearly not only a matter of style).

The following three passages, each containing about a hundred words, respectively represent informal, more formal and scientific styles. Notice how the number of French, Latin and Greek elements gradually increases:

«Well, that was where I found myself on my wedding night. Hugh and I disliked each other on sight, and Jimmy knew it. He was so proud of us both, so *pathetically anxious* that we should take to each other. Like a child showing off his toys. We had a little wedding *celebration*, and the three of us tried to get tight on some cheap port they'd brought in. Hugh got more and more *subtly insulting* -he'd a *rare talent* for that. Jimmy got steadily *depressed*, and I *just* sat there, listening to their talk, looking and feeling very *stupid*. For the first time in my life, I was cut off from the kind of *people* I'd always known, *family*, my friends, everybody».

(Osborne, Look Back in Anger)

«Everyone will *agree* that this has been a long *Parliament*. We need not *embark* on *historical controversy* as to the *claims* to *continuous* life which could be put forward on behalf of a *Parliament* much longer than this, but I am *very* glad that the *closing session* of this long ten years' *Parliament* should show all the *due respect* for the *traditional* and *ceremonial occasions* which *ignorant*, unthinking *people* who have not *meditated* upon these *matters* or *studied* the true *movement* of *events* and of *forces* in the *human* breast might *easily regard* as meaningless *punctilio*. Here in the Speech from the *Throne* and in the *debate* on the *Address* may be seen all the workings.»

(Churchill, Speech in the Commons)

«*Fiber-optics cables represent* a new *technology* that is rewriting the speed *records* for the *transmission* of *voice*, *data* and *video communications*. These *cables*, sending *vast* chunks of *information* in *pulses* of light, *signify* more than an *incremental advance* in *telecommunications engineering*. They *provide extraordinary capabilities just* beginning to be *recognized* outside the *telecommunications industry*. New York *Governor* Mario Cuomo, who has spoken of the *potential power* of *fiber-optics cables* to *energize* the *economies* of *different regions*, calls them «the *rail*road tracks of the 198Os», likening them to the *installation* of the first *transcontinental* tracks as a way to *deliver* the goods -in this *case*, bits of *information*.

(R.Corrigan, Fiber Optics)

Compare, in the following lists, the French items with their two translation equivalents, one of Latin or French origin and characteristic of a more formal level of language, the other of more everyday usage:

-nouns:	F.	*aide*	E. *aid*	*help*
		amitié	*amity*	*friendship*
		chance	*fortune*	*luck*
		commerce	*commerce*	*trade*
		époux, épouse	*spouse*	*husband, wife*
		fatigue	*fatigue*	*tiredness*
		liberté	*liberty*	*freedom*
		menace	*menace*	*threat*
		présent	*present*	*gift*
		réponse	*response*	*answer*
verbs:	F.	*acheter*	E. *to purchase*	*to buy*
		assembler	*to assemble*	*to meet*
		commencer	*to commence*	*to begin*
		désirer	*to desire*	*to wish*
		éjecter	*to eject*	*to throw out*
		entrer	*to enter*	*to go in*
		éteindre	*to extinguish*	*to put out*
		fonctionner	*to function*	*to work*
		habiter	*to inhabit*	*to live in*
		recevoir	*to receive*	*to get*
		remettre	*to postpone*	*to put off*
		saisir	*to seize*	*to take*
adjectives:				
	F.	*aigu (douleur)*	E. *acute*	*sharp*
		aimable	*amiable*	*friendly*
		céleste	*celestial*	*heavenly*
		cordial	*cordial*	*hearty*
		érudit	*erudite*	*learned*
		erroné	*erroneous*	*false*
		fraternel	*fraternal*	*brotherly*
		maternel	*maternal*	*motherly*
		mortel	*mortal*	*deadly*
		nocturne	*nocturnal*	*nightly*
		obscure	*obscure*	*dark*
		profond	*profound*	*deep*
		prudent	*prudent*	*careful*
		solitaire	*solitary*	*lonely*

In some cases, however, the opposite is true, and the Germanic item is less colloquial (often more poetic) than the one of French origin:

F.	*action*	E. *action*	*deed*
	crucifix	*crucifix*	*rood*
	ennemi	*enemy*	*foe*

pays	*country*	*land*
faire attention à	*to pay attention to*	*to heed*
récompenser	*to reward*	*to meed*
vallée	*valley*	*dale*

I.4. TRANSLATIONAL EQUIVALENCE IS ONLY PARTIAL FROM A COLLOCATIONAL POINT OF VIEW

Collocational meaning was defined in I.7 of Part One as the meaning of a word as far as it is determined by the preferential or exclusive company it keeps. As such preferential or exclusive co-occurrence cannot be accounted for on conceptual or rational grounds, but is simply a matter of the usage characteristics of individual words, it raises problems of equivalence which the foreign learner may have serious trouble coping with. It also raises problems for the contrastive linguist, who finds himself in an area where language-specific idiosyncracy is the rule and where no generalisations can be made.He can do little more than point out the phenomena, though in the case of English and French he will again be struck by the richness of the English vocabulary, where the existence of larger groups of near-synonymous words seems to correlate with a larger number of specific co-occurrences.

A few examples may be added to the ones given in I.7 of Part One:

F. *faire* :	E. *make*, *do*, *take*, *have*, *give*, *cook*
les lits :	*to make the beds*
les chambres:	*to do the rooms*
la lessive :	*to do the laundry*
du café, du thé:	*to make coffee, tea*
de la soupe :	*to make soup*
un repas :	*to cook a meal*
un exercice :	*to do an exercise*
un examen :	*to do, to take an exam*
une conférence:	*to give a lecture*
de la recherche:	*to do research*
une promenade :	*to have, to take a walk* (also *to go for*)
une excursion :	*to take a trip* (also *to go on*)
l'amour :	*to make love*
la guerre :	*to make war*

un plaisir :	*to do a favour*
des affaires :	*to do business*
F. *devenir* :	E. *become, get, go, grow, turn, run*
vieux :	*to become, to get, to grow old*
gros :	*to become, to get, to grow fat*
pâle :	*to become, to go, to grow, to turn pale*
silencieux :	*to become, to grow silent*
célèbre :	*to become, to get famous*
grand :	*to get, to grow tall*
comme fou :	*to go, to run wild*
fou :	*to go mad*
rouge :	*to turn red*
F. *beau, joli* :	E. *beautiful, handsome, pretty, good-looking*
homme :	*a handsome, good-looking man*
femme :	*a beautiful, pretty, good-looking woman*
chien :	*a beautiful, handsome, (pretty) dog*
fleur :	*a beautiful, pretty flower*
village :	*a beautiful, pretty village*
robe :	*a beautiful, pretty dress*
cadeau :	*a beautiful, handsome present*
voiture :	*a beautiful, handsome car*
avion :	*a beautiful, handsome plane*
pardessus :	*a beautiful overcoat*
E. *to meet, to satisfy*:	F. *payer, régler, faire face à, s'acquitter de, combler, satisfaire, répondre à, remplir*
the bill :	*payer, régler la note*
the expenses :	*faire face aux dépenses*
a debt :	*s'acquitter d'une dette*
a demand :	*satisfaire à, répondre à une exigence*
a deficit :	*combler un déficit*
a condition :	*remplir une condition*
E. *to experience, to suffer*:	F. *connaître, essuyer, souffrir, rencontrer, éprouver*
a serious crisis :	*connaître une crise grave*
insults :	*essuyer des insultes*
hardships :	*souffrir des privations*
ill-treatment :	*subir un mauvais traitement*

difficulties :	*rencontrer des difficultés*
difficulty in... :	*éprouver de la difficulté à...*

E. *a fit*:	F. *accès, attaque, quinte, crise, poussée, transport*
of anger :	*un accès de colère*
of hysterics :	*attaque de nerfs*
of coughing :	*une quinte de toux*
of crying :	*une crise de larmes*
of jealousy :	*transports de jalousie*

CHAPTER II: DECEPTIVE COGNATES (faux amis)

So far we have been interested exclusively in contrasting the meanings of related English and French words, without paying attention to their forms. However, perhaps the most striking thing about the English and French vocabularies is first of all that so many words have an identical or similar spelling form [1](*crime*:*crime*, *river*:*rivière*, *to deceive*:*décevoir*) and, secondly, that whereas some of these pairs of items have the same meaning content, the large majority are deceptive cognates or faux amis in that they are either only partially equivalent or totally non-equivalent from a semantic point of view. It seems pedagogically useful therefore to devote our final chapter to the problems raised by formally similar words, even if partially deceptive cognates have in fact already been dealt with implicitly, in that the previous chapter was devoted to partial equivalence of meaning without discriminating between formally different and formally similar items.

II.1. COMMON WORDS AND COGNATES

If the term « common words » is reserved for all English and French words that are identical or similar in form, the following distinctions ought to be made:

1° purely incidental homonyms (« rencontres homonymiques bilingues », as Darbelnet (1973) calls them). They are pairs such as *chat* :*chat*, *son* : *son*, *pain* : *pain* etc., which have no etymological link and as a rule belong to quite distinct semantic areas, often also to different word-classes (*but* : *but*).

2° direct borrowings from Latin and from Greek in English, mostly as a result of the systematic christianisation of Britain in the VIIth century, of the prestige of Latin all through the Middle Ages, but especially of the revival of classical learning in the XVIth and XVIIth centuries. *Angel*, *candle*, *martyr*, *psalm*, *stole*, *temple* and many other words to do with religion go back to the first period, as do a considerable number of items related to education and learning (*school*, *master*, *verse*, *circle*, *talent*, etc.) or to everyday life (*cap*, *pine*, *radish*,

---

1 See Appendix I for some critical spelling differences.

trout, etc.). The later borrowings found their way to English through the writings of churchmen, scholars and poets. Frequent words such as *contempt*, *custody*, *genius*, *gesture*, *history*, *include*, *individual*, *infinite*, *intellect*, *interrupt*, *legal*, *moderate*, *nervous*, *polite*, *popular*, *quiet*, *spacious*, *submit*, *temporal* and *testify* were adopted at the end of the Middle Ages; other items, e.g. *adapt*, *alienate*, *assassinate*, *consist*, *exact*, *exaggerate*, *exert*, *expensive*, *extinguish*, *habitual*, *ingenuity*, *insane*, *meditate* and *pretext*, during the Renaissance. The number of these loan-words is very considerable, though it must be pointed out that it is often impossible to determine whether a given item was borrowed directly from Latin or indirectly from Latin through French -or whether there was influence from both languages at the same time.

3° English words borrowed from French. These represent the large majority of common words and, together with the items referred to in the previous section, over 30% of the total vocabulary of English.

A massive influx of French words occurred in the centuries following the Norman Conquest (1066), when many French noblemen chose to take up residence in Britain and filled the important positions there. For two centuries French was the language of social prestige, adopted by the upper classes and gradually but massively infiltrating the English vocabulary. The lexical areas affected are naturally those that were the élite's chief concern: government and administration (*administer*, *govern*, *empire*, *authority*, *majesty*, *royal*, *court*, *governor*, *mayor*, *noble*, *prince*, *duke*, *count*, etc.), the church (*religion*, *sermon*, *baptism*, *clergy*, *vicar*, etc.), legal matters (*justice*, *crime*, *proof*, *judge*, *sentence*, *ransom*, *prison*, *innocent*, etc.), art and learning (*art*, *beauty*, *music*, *poet*, *colour*, *study*, *grammar*, *gender*, *medicine*, *remedy*, *stomach*, *astronomy*, *geometry*, etc.), fashion and social life (*fashion*, *brooch*, *button*, *buckle*, *boot*, *diamond*, *pearl*; *dinner*, *supper*, *feast*, *appetite*, *beef*, *pork*, *mutton*, *cream*, *sugar*, *fruit*, *peach*, *plate*, *mirror*, *wardrobe*, etc.). In some cases the loan-words of this period were «unnecessary», in the sense that they did not fill a gap in the English vocabulary, so that they had to compete with already existing, synonymous items. The new word might then discard the old one: *ēam*, *here*, *lof*, *aeþele*, *earm*, *belīfan*, for example, disappeared when the romance items *uncle*, *army*, *praise*, *noble*, *poor* and *remain* were introduced. But in most cases the adoption of a romance «synonym» resulted in semantic differentiation, as described in II.3 below.

As the cultural, political and economic relations between France and England have been close all through history, the introduction of French words into the English vocabulary continued in more recent times. They belong to a great variety of areas: diplomacy, military life, trade, the arts, cuisine, and social life in general. *Envoy*, *colonel*, *brigade*, *platoon*, *invoice*, *crayon*, *scene*, *memoirs*, *menu*, *soup*, *liqueur*, *genteel*, *madame*, *liaison*, *naive* are only a very small sample.

A distinction ought to be made between the loan-words so far mentioned, which are on the whole fully anglicized and have therefore usually undergone changes of meaning and form, and « gallicisms », i.e. items introduced at a much more recent date, which have retained their French form and meaning and are clearly felt as foreign. A few examples are *apéritif*, *concierge*, *discothèque*, *au courant*, *enfant terrible*, *idée fixe*, *nouveau riche*, *raison d'être*, *joie de vivre*, *bête noire*. They often find their origin in the mannerism of a social group and may therefore be short-lived.

4° French words borrowed from English. Of those that have been fully adapted or « naturalized », some go back to Middle English: *bateau*, *nord*, *sud*, *est* and *ouest*, for instance, respectively from *batil*, *north*, *suth*, *east*, *west*. Many others, such as e.g. *parlement*, *jury*, *budget*, *club*, *congrès*, *voter*, *jockey*, *boxe*, *punch* and *pudding*, were introduced in the XVIIIth century. But it is in the XIXth century that large numbers of English words start invading the various areas of the French vocabulary: sport (*football*, *golf*, *tennis*, *hockey*, etc.), technical domains (*wagon*, *tunnel*, *ballast*, *film*, etc.), social life (*hall*, *palace*, *confort*, *flirt*, etc.), food and drink (*sandwich*, *bifteck*, *whisky*, *cocktail*, etc.). Of more recent date, and often described as « anglicisms » or simply as « mots anglais », are such items as *boom*, *building*, *camping*, *container*, *dancing*, *dealer*, *design*, *drugstore*, *ferry*, *finish*, *gentleman*, *footing*, *home*, *interview*, *jet*, *lunch*, *marketing*, *manager*, *milkshake*, *motel*, *overdrive*, *planning*, *shopping*, *sweater*, *snack*, *walkman* or *week-end*.

It is worth noting that some lexical items have gone back and forth, i.e.were first borrowed in English from the French language, then disappeared in French but were later reintroduced from English. *Budget* (from Middle French *bougette*, diminutive form of *bouge*= sac, valise) is a case in point, as are *square* (from Old French *esquarre*= carré), *bacon*, *bar*, *festival*, *reporter*, *sport*, *suspense*, etc.

Although the percentage of English loan-words in the productive vocabulary of French is relatively low (2, 5% according to a recent count), and although some of them are short-lived (will the present-day use of *zapping*, *des basket*, *cool* or *le look* survive our generation?), their number tends to increase. « De langue prêteuse, le français est devenu une langue emprunteuse », says Gebhart (1975), and anglo-americanisms represent by far the largest part of these « emprunts ». As many French intellectuals feel that this influx gradually saps the genius of the French language (cfr. Etiemble's well-known book

«Parlez-vous franglais?», 1964), legal action has been taken against it in France.

5° Words borrowed from a third language by both English and French (and often by many other languages as well), generally in the original form. *Fiasco*, *scenario* (from Italian), *goulash*, *paprika* (from Hungarian), *leitmotiv*, *ersatz* (from German), and *apartheid* (from Afrikaans) are a few such items.

6° Scientific compounds formed from Latin and Greek elements, usually shared by the languages of many developed speech communities: *telephone*, *television*, *telescope*, *microfilm*, *autograph*, *pesticide*, *phonology*, *thermonuclear*, etc.

Of these different categories of common words, the first one is of relatively little interest from a linguistic and pedagogical point of view. For if formally similar words have nothing in common from the point of view of their origin, they will often belong to different word-classes and almost certainly to quite distinct areas of meaning. They will therefore occur in totally different linguistic contexts and rarely mislead the learner, except perhaps in the very first stages of the learning process.

Categories 5 and 6 consist almost exclusively of «international» words, i.e. words shared not only by English and French, but by most languages used for educational and technical purposes.

It is the remaining categories (2, 3 and 4) that contain the most interesting pairs from a contrastive point of view and for which we shall reserve the term «cognates». The deceptiveness of these cognates is a result of the conditions in which one item of the pair was borrowed, and of the specific semantic development the two cognates have undergone in their languages.

II.2. DECEPTIVENESS AS A RESULT OF BORROWING

When a lexical item is borrowed from another language, it will as a rule be formally adapted, i.e. phonetically, but often also graphically and morphologically. If *crime* and *crime*, *figure* and *figure* differ only from the point of view of pronunciation, little is left of the formal link between E.*(hand)kerchief* and F.*couvre-chef*, E.*curfew* and F.*couvre-feu*, or F.*redingote* and E.*riding-coat*, F.*boulingrin* and E.*bowling-green*. But let us leave problems of formal adaptation aside and focus on some phenomena which account for the semantic deceptiveness of cognates.

Occasionally a language borrows a word in a sense in which it is not used in the donor language, thus creating a deceptive pair. This is the case, for example, with such French loan-words as *car*, *chips*, *cross*, *pull*, *snack*, *slip*, *speaker*, and many items in *-ing* (*brushing*, *camping*, *footing*, *living*, *sleeping*, *smoking*. What these recent borrowings refer to is expressed in English respectively by *coach*, *crisps*, *cross-country*, *pullover*, *snack-bar*, *pant(ie)s* or *(swimming) trunks*, *announcer*, *blow-dry*, *camp site* (or *camping ground*, *camping place*), *walking*, *living room*, *sleeping car*, *dinner jacket*. In some of these cases it is in fact unjustified to speak of «borrowing»: *footing* and other items in *-ing*, for instance, have simply been made up on the pattern of the well-known *-ing* form in *swimming*, *touring*, etc.; the same applies to such compounds as *auto-stop*, *recordman* or *baby-foot*, totally unknown to speakers of English (who use *hitch-hiking*, *record holder* and *table football*), but modelled after existing English patterns (*bus stop*, *policeman*, *baby car*).

Words which have only one sense, usually a specialized or technical one, will be borrowed and as a rule maintained in this one sense by the recipient language. This applies, for instance, to the large number of sports terms the French language owes to English (*bobsleigh*, *bookmaker*, *hockey*, *knock-out*, *sprint*, *lob*, etc.), and to the cooking terms which English has taken over from French (*apéritif*, *mayonnaise*, *rosé*, etc.), which are therefore «bons amis» for the learner of the other language.

Non-specialized or non-technical words, however, which are almost invariably polysemous in the donor language, are usually borrowed in one of their senses only. Some of them preserve this one meaning, as recent loans such as E.*atelier*, *bourgeois*, *chef*, *cuisine* or F.*match*, *smash*, *rally* or *bar* have so far done, and are thus deceptive cognates because of their monosemy. But as a rule the loan-word will start a new life in the new language, independently of the original language, i.e.take on new meanings and/or adjust to the new lexical system at the cost of conceptual, connotative, stylistic or collocational differentiation (See II.3 below). It naturally follows that non-specialized or non-technical cognates are almost invariably deceptive from one or other of these points of view. Some of the examples traditionally cited in textbooks are nouns such as *abuse:abus*, *agreement: agrément*, *argument: argument*, *barracks: baraque*, *cave: cave*, *corpse: corps*, *costume: costume*, *delay: délai*, *figure: figure*, *injury: injure*, *journal: journal*, *lecture: lecture*, *library: librairie*, *opportunity: opportunité*, *phrase: phrase*, *response: réponse*, *vacancy: vacance(s)*, verbs such as *to achieve: achever*, *to attend: attendre*, *to charge: charger*, *to deceive: décevoir*, *to demand: demander*, *to dispose: disposer*, *to introduce: introduire*, *to pretend: prétendre*, *to realize: réaliser*, adjectives such as *actual: actuel*, *brave: brave*, *eventual: éventuel*, *genial: génial*, *large: large*, *sensible: sensible*, *sympathetic: sympathique*, but they represent of course only a tiny sample.

The distinction which is traditionally made between totally and partially deceptive cognates concerns only conceptual meaning content: cognates are either totally deceptive (viz. when their conceptual meanings totally diverge) or partially deceptive (viz. when they share one or more conceptual meanings). In the latter case there may be inclusion (viz. when the semantic space of one cognate is included in that of the other), or overlapping (viz. when there is a common semantic space, but specific extensions of meaning for both cognates). The examples given on the following page and taken from the «Dictionnaire des faux amis anglais-français» (J.Van Roey, S.Granger and H.Swallow, 1988) illustrate these cases: *injure:injury* are totally deceptive cognates; *bouton:button*, *fraude:fraud* and *rivière:river* are partially deceptive, with the first two pairs representing cases of inclusion, the last one a case of overlapping.

As the meaning content of the cognate may also change in the donor language after borrowing has taken place, there are many cases where the English loan-word has kept the meaning expressed by the French or Latin cognate at the time of borrowing. Thus the meanings of the English words *to alter*, *to deceive*, *to demand*, *to labour*, *library* or *to resume* are the original meanings of the corresponding words in French, where they have taken on a different sense in the course of time, or in Latin. This phenomenon is probably to be attributed to the fact that words of romance origin are on the whole of less everyday use in English and therefore less exposed to semantic change.

II.3. THE NATURE OF THE DECEPTIVENESS

Basically, the semantic differences between deceptive cognates are of the same general kinds as the differences observed between so-called translation equivalents: conceptual, connotative, stylistic and collocational. In fact, as we have pointed out, some of the partial translation equivalents dealt with in Chapter One of Part Two are cognates, so that the object of this paragraph has already been partially covered.(See for instance the description of the stylistic difference between F.*aide* and E.*aid*, F.*menace* and E.*menace* in Part Two, I.3). But the specific meaning differences between deceptive cognates are worth studying in themselves, as has been shown by H.Chuquet & M.Paillard (1987) and by S.Granger & H.Swallow (1988), to whom we owe some of the observations and examples below.

INJURE / INJURY

II	1.	Il considéra ces paroles comme une **injure** personnelle	He took these words as a personal **insult**
		Quand son mari avait bu, il l'accablait d'**injures**	When her husband had been drinking he would shower **abuse** *(nd)* on her
III	2.	Fortunately his **injuries** were not severe	Heureusement, ses **blessures** n'étaient pas graves

BOUTON / BUTTON

I	1.	Pourrais-tu me coudre ce **bouton** ?	Could you sew this **button** on for me ?
	2.	Quand on pousse sur ce **bouton**, l'enregistreur se met en marche	When you press this **button** the tape recorder starts
II	3.	J'ai un horrible **bouton** sur le nez et je dois passer à la télévision ce soir	I've got a horrible **spot/pimple** on my nose and I'm on television this evening
	4.	Les roses sont déjà en **bouton**	The roses are already in **bud**

FRAUDE / FRAUD

I	1.	*(Jur)* Ce banquier a été reconnu coupable de **fraude**. Il vendait des actions qui n'avaient aucune valeur	The banker was found guilty of **fraud**. He had been selling shares worth nothing at all
III	2.	That man's a **fraud** ! He's no more an earl than I am !	Cet homme est un **imposteur**. Il n'est pas plus comte que moi !
		This slimming cream's a **fraud** ! I haven't lost an inch round the waist	Cette crème amincissante est un **attrape-nigaud**. Je n'ai pas perdu un centimètre de tour de taille
		This reform programme is a massive **fraud** !	Ce programme de réformes est une vaste **fumisterie** * !

RIVIÈRE / RIVER

I	1.	Il est parfois dangereux de se baigner dans une **rivière**	It's sometimes dangerous to bathe in a **river** ⇨ 3
II	2.	*(Hippisme)* Il ne reste plus au dernier concurrent qu'à passer le mur et la **rivière**	The final competitor only has to clear the wall and the **water jump**
III	3.	The Amazon is the largest **river** in the world	L'Amazone est le plus grand **fleuve** du monde

II.3.1.CONCEPTUAL

From the standpoint of conceptual meaning, it is first of all clear that the total denotational scope of a cognate (i.e.the semantic space covered by its senses) will in general be wider in the French language than in the English language if the cognate is of French origin, and vice versa. This is simply because, as stated, languages as a rule borrow words in one specific sense only. Even if there is a subsequent extension of the meaning of the loan-word in the recipient language, the cognate will nevertheless usually be more polysemous in the donor language, where it has led a longer life. This no doubt applies to French loan-words in English: in many cases they belong to a more intellectual or even more formal or specialized register, so that they will be less exposed to the extension of meaning characteristic of everyday words. If, in addition, one considers that most pairs of cognates are of French origin, it is only natural that the French item will frequently be more polysemous than its English «twin».

If we turn our attention from the total denotational scope to the separate senses of cognates, we notice that the cognitive differences between comparable senses may range from very slight nuances to considerable divergence and even to near-oppositeness of meaning.

Examples of subtle distinctions are, amongst many others:

E.*ancient* :	of a very distant past
F.*ancien* :	of a very distant or more recent past (e.g.une chanson ancienne : an old song)
E.*to announce* :	to make known publicly
F.*annoncer* :	to make known, to tell (e.g.il m'a annoncé que : he told me that...)
E.*delicious* :	pleasing to taste or smell
F.*délicieux* :	giving great pleasure (e.g.un endroit délicieux : a charming, delightful place)
E.*to finish* :	to come to an end (in a temporal sense)
F.*finir* :	to come to an end (in a temporal or spatial sense) (e.g.le sentier finissait là : the path ended there)
E.*important* :	of qualitative significance
F.*important* :	of qualitative or quantitative significance (e.g.une somme importante : a large sum of money)

More marked divergence or, in some cases, near-oppositeness may be illustrated by

E.*to pretend* :	to make oneself appear to be
F.*prétendre* :	to claim
E.*versatile* :	having many different kinds of skill
F.*versatile* :	changeable, fickle, capricious
E.*sensible* :	reasonable, having good sense
F.*sensible* :	sensitive, tender-hearted
E.*patron* :	client, customer
F.*patron* :	boss
E.*truculent* :	defiant and aggressive
F.*truculent* :	vivid, colourful
E.*petulant* :	showing (childish) bad temper
F.*pétulant* :	exuberant, vivacious
E.*mundane* :	ordinary and typically unexciting
F.*mondain* :	relating to fashionable society
E.*to dispose of* :	to get rid of
F.*disposer de* :	to possess, to have at one's disposal

The conceptual differences between the individual senses of English and French faux amis to some extent fall into the categories traditionally distinguished for semantic change (See Part One, I.8). By this we mean that phenomena such as specialisation of meaning, which may be observed when making a diachronic study of the meanings of a word in one and the same language (for instance the meaning of OE.*deor* (=animal) and that of its modern form *deer* (=a specific animal)), may also account for the semantic difference between, for instance, F.*annoncer* (=to make known) and E.*to announce* (=to make known publicly), even if the term «change» cannot usually be taken in the strict historical sense, so that the term «difference» may be more suitable.

Some such differences are:

1.The sense of the cognate in the recipient language is either narrower or more specialized than in the donor language or, more rarely, wider or more generalized. The slight cognitive differences between the pairs mentioned above (*ancient* : *ancien*, *to announce* : *annoncer*, *delicious* : *délicieux*, *to finish* : *finir*, *important* : *important*) in fact illustrate the specialisation of the English loan-word, as do

F.*assassiner* :	to murder
E.*assassinate* :	to murder for political reasons

F.*bal* :	dance
E.*ball* :	formal dance
F.*bouquet* :	bunch of flowers
E.*bouquet* :	bunch of flowers carefully arranged
F.*costume* :	set of outer garments
E.*costume* :	set of outer garments worn on the stage
F.*étranger* :	a person unfamiliar or from a foreign country
E.*stranger* :	a person who is unfamiliar
F.*marcher* :	to walk
E.*to march* :	to walk in a military way
F.*saluer* :	to greet
E.*to salute* :	to greet in a military way

Similarly, the sense of French words borrowed from English will as a rule be more specialized:

E.*fuel* :	wood, coal, oil, gas
F.*fuel* :	heating oil
E.*green* :	smooth stretch of grass for games, dances etc.
F.*green* :	grassy part of a golf course
E.*leader* :	person who guides or directs a group
F.*leader* :	person who guides or directs a political group or movement

Occasionally the opposite is true: the sense of the cognate in the recipient language is wider or more generalized than in the donor language:

F.*altérer* :	to become or make different and less good
E.*to alter* :	to become or make different
F.*carpette* :	small floor covering
E.*carpet* :	floor covering
F.*crime* :	very serious offence punishable by law
E.*crime* :	offence punishable by law

2.The meaning of the cognate in the recipient language is either more appreciative or less appreciative than in the donor language (amelioration, deterioration). The former is the case in the first two examples, the latter in the last four:

F.*luxure* :	lust
E.*luxury* :	great comfort
F.*truand* :	gangster, mobster, crook
E.*truant* :	pupil staying away from school
F.*juvenile* :	young
E.*juvenile* :	immature and foolish
F.*mignon* :	pretty, sweet
E.*minion* (n.):	servile person
F.*promiscuité* :	crowding
E.*promiscuity* :	loose sexual behaviour
F.*petit* :	small
E.*petty* :	trivial, unimportant, mean

3.The sense of the cognate in the recipient language denotes a higher degree of intensity in the quality expressed by the adjective or in the activity expressed by the verb:

F.*grave*	
E.*grave* :	very serious
F.*brutal*	
E.*brutal* :	violent, cruel
F.*demander*	
E.*to demand* :	to claim as if by right
F.*interroger*	
E.*interrogate* :	to question aggressively or closely and for some time

4.The sense of the cognate adjective in the recipient language denotes either a more temporary or a more permanent characteristic than in the donor language:

F.*nerveux* :	permanent or temporary
E.*nervous* :	permanent (except in the sense of « apprehensive », « fearful », « uneasy »)
F.*sauf* :	temporary
E.*safe* :	permanent
F.*franc* :	permanent or temporary
E.*frank* :	temporary

F.*sobre* :	permanent (or temporary)
E.*sober* :	temporary

5.The sense of the cognate is figurative in the recipient language. Cases of metonymy may be distinguished from metaphor:

F.	*flannelle*	E.	*flannels* (trousers made of flannel)
	chapelle		*chapel* (religious service)
	étude		*study* (room used for study and work)
	fraude		*fraud* (deceitful person)
	charité		*charity* (charitable institution)

E.	*dancing*	F.	*dancing* (place for dancing)
	parking		*parking* (space for parking)
	cargo		*cargo* (cargo boat)

F.	*bonnet*	E.	*bonnet* (of a car)
	branche		*branch* (of a river)
	épine		*spine* (of a book)
	finir		*to finish* (a person = to exhaust)
	immaculé		*immaculate* (=perfect)
	plonger		*to plunge* (=to drop suddenly)
	touche		*a touch* (of sadness = small amount)
	veine		*a vein* (of truth = small amount)

II.3.2. CONNOTATIVE

Apart from these conceptual differences, specific connotative features may also account for the deceptiveness of English and French cognates (exactly as they may in the case of any so-called translation equivalents: see Part One, I.5).

In the pairs F.*luxure* : E.*luxury*, F.*truand* : E.*truant* etc. just described, a depreciative or appreciative feature was a distinctive, essential element of the meaning of one of the cognates. In other cases, however, some such conceptual or emotive feature only tends to be associated with what a cognate denotes in one of the two languages, and is thus deceptive to speakers of the other language.

In several pairs one of the cognates has a pejorative connotation whereas the other one is neutral (or even ameliorative). Thus, while F.*politicien*, *populace*, *routine* and *individu* connote pejoratively, their English twins *politician*, *populace* and *routine* are neutral (and *individual* usually is).

II.3.3.STYLISTIC

It is probably from the point of view of style that French learners of English are most often led astray in the use of cognates. It has been pointed out on more than one occasion so far that the quantitative superiority of the English lexicon and some of its specific qualities are to a considerable extent due to the massive adoption of French and Latin words. As already mentioned, this has frequently resulted in the existence in English of Germanic-Romance doublets (*help*:*aid*, *get*:*obtain*), synonymous from a conceptual point of view but of different stylistic value, whereby the Germanic item is as a rule more everyday, the Romance item more intellectual, technical or formal. As French learners will, in the case of such doublets, quite naturally tend to use the item that is evoked by the French cognate, errors of a stylistic order are extremely frequent.

Examples of stylistically deceptive cognates are legion and the reader is referred to I.3 for numerous cases illustrating the formal/informal contrast. Perhaps we may, in the same context, mention the well-known sociolinguistic phenomenon whereby foreign words are used as a status symbol. Thus *maître d'hôtel*, *chambré*, *frappé*, *lingerie*, *savoir faire*, and other such recent borrowings are preferred by some English speakers to *headwaiter*, *brought to room temperature*, *well-chilled*, *underwear*, *know-how* because of the «chic français» they convey (See Chirol 1973). Similarly, the use of such anglicisms as *le footing*, *le shopping*, *le show-biz*, *le design*, *le feed-back*, *le look* give the French speaker the prestige of being «in». Cognates are thus created -but deceptive ones, for the chic or prestige is of course absent in the original language.

With regard to the opposition technical /non-technical, consider the following cases, where a stylistically unmarked French item corresponds to two English words, one in common use, the other a cognate belonging to technical or scientific style:

F.	*microbe*	E.	*germ* *microbe* (Med.)
	clavicule		*collarbone* *clavicle* (Med.)
	tympan		*eardrum* *tympan(um)* (Med.)
	domicile		*home* *domicile* (Admin.)
	antenne		*aerial*

	antenna (Techn.)
orthographe	*spelling* *orthography* (Ling.)

Cognates may also be deceptive because they represent a geographical variety, as in

F.	*bagages*	E.	*baggage* (US) *luggage* (Brit.)
	appartement		*apartment* (US) *flat* (Brit.)
	aubergine		*aubergine* (Brit.) *eggplant* (US)
	autumn		*autumn* (Brit.) *fall* (US)

II.3.4. COLLOCATIONAL

A final but far from minor source of error is to be found in the specific collocational restraints cognates are subject to. A lexical item will combine into a syntactic pattern with certain lexical items to the exclusion of others, whereas its cognate will not show comparable restrictions. In Part One, I.7 and Part Two, I.4 the phenomenon was discussed and illustrated, so that a few further examples specifically concerning deceptive cognates may suffice:

F. *composer*	E. *to compose*
un menu	a menu
un texte	a text
une symphonie	a symphony
un programme	*to work out* a programme
un plat	*to make up* a dish
une équipe	*to select* a team
un numéro de téléphone	*to dial* a telephone number

F. *correspondre*	E. *to correspond*
à une description	to a description
au goût de qqn	*to suit* someone's taste
aux capacités de qqn	*to fit* someone's capacities
à la réalité	*to square* with reality
au désir de qqn	*to meet, to answer* so's wish

F. un photographe *professionnel*	E. a *professional* photographer
une maladie *professionnelle*	an *occupational* disease

une formation *professionnelle*	*vocational* training
déformation *professionnelle*	*job* conditioning
soucis *professionnels*	*work* problems
faute *professionnelle*	*malpractice* (Med.)

F. *fausse* barbe	E. *false* beard
fausses dents	*false* teeth
faux plafond	*false* ceiling
fausse fenêtre	*blind* window
fausse monnaie	*forged* currency

APPENDIX I

SOME CRITICAL SPELLING DIFFERENCES IN "COMMON WORDS"

FRENCH	ENGLISH		
a	ad	amiral	admiral
		avancer	advance
		avantage	advantage
		Avent	Advent
		aventure	adventure
		(avocat)	advocate
ance	ence	correspondance	correspondence
		(in)dépendance	(in)dependence
		insistance	insistence
		persistance	persistence
		subsistance	subsistence
ant	ent	constituant	constituent
		correspondant	correspondent
		délinquant	delinquent
		inconsistant	inconsistent
		(in)dépendant	(in)dependent
		insistant	insistent
		persistant	persistent
c	k	(blanc)	blank
		clerc	clerk
		flanc	flank
		parc	park
		(porc)	pork
c	ck	bloc	block
		choc	shock
		coucou	cuckoo
c	s	exercice	exercise
		maçon	mason
		parcimonieux	parsimonious
c	ch	caractère	character
		(corde)	chord
		mécanicien	mechanic

		mélancolie	melancholy
		scolastique	scholastic
ch	sh	châle	shawl
		choc	shock
		maréchal	marshal
f	ff	girafe	giraffe
		safran	saffron
		tarif	tariff
		trafic	traffic
f	ph	fantôme	phantom
		faisan	pheasant
		flegme	phlegm
f	ve	décisif	decisive
		infinitif	infinitive
		génitif	genitive
		motif	motive
		négatif	negative
		nerf	nerve
g	dg	juge	judge
		loge	lodge
g	gg	agrégation	aggregation
		agresseur	aggressor
		agressif	aggressive
		droguiste	druggist
		exagérer	exaggerate
		hagard	haggard
i	e	chimiste	chemist
		limonade	lemonade
i	y	baie	bay
		célerie	celery
		quai	quay
l	ll	bal	ball
		balistique	ballistic
		controleur	controller
		(galant)	gallant
		galerie	gallery
		galop	gallop
		modeleur	modeller
		pâleur	pallor
		pilori	pillory
		(vilain)	villain

ll	l	assaillant	assailant
		balle	bale
		bataillon	battalion
		sollicitude	solicitude
		périlleux	perilous
		pavillon	pavilion
		vaillant	valiant
		vermillon	vermilion
m	mm	comité	committee
		maman	mamma
		(a)symétrie	symmetry
mm	m	dommage	damage
		hommage	homage
		pommade	pomade
n	m	confort	comfort
		rançon	ransom
		Sanson	Samson
n	nn	flanelle	flannel
		canon	cannon
		dîner	dinner
nn	n	conditionnel	conditional
		exceptionnel	exceptional
		personnel	personal
		sensationnel	sensational
		dictionnaire	dictionary
		millionnaire	millionaire
		stationnaire	stationary
		visionnaire	visionary
		baïonnette	bayonet
		ennemi	enemy
		espionnage	espionage
		pionnier	pioneer
o	u	abondant	abundant
		circonstance	circumstance
		colonne	column
		inonder	inundate
		onduler	undulate
		ponctuel	punctual
		volontaire	voluntary
		volontaire(s.)	volunteer
pp	p	appartement	apartment
		développé	developed

		développement	development
		enveloppe	envelope
		rapport	report
r	rr	(baraque)	barracks
		carotte	carrot
		miroir	mirror
		mariage	marriage
		baril	barrel
rr	r	carrière	career
		courrier	courier
		fourrage	forage
re	er	membre	member
		monstre	monster
		neutre	neuter
		offre	offer
		sinistre	sinister
		sobre	sober
		tendre	tender
s	z	Brésil	Brazil
		Elisabeth	Elizabeth
		(hasard)	hazard
		maïs	maize
s	ss	accès	access
		procès	process
		succès	success
ss	s	(bassin)	basin
		pressentiment	presentiment
		ressembler	resemble
		ressentiment	resentment
		ressource	resource
t	th	auteur	author
		diphtongue	diphthong
		trône	throne
t	ct	conflit	conflict
		contrat	contract
		effet	effect
		objet	object
		pratique	practical
		préfet	prefect
		projet	project
		refléter	reflect
		sujet	subject

t	tt	bouton	button
		coton	cotton
		glouton	glutton
tt	t	carotte	carrot
		littéraire	literary
		littéral	literal
		littérature	literature
		mascotte	mascot
		polyglotte	polyglot
-	e	candidat	candidate
		chocolat	chocolate
		délicat	delicate
		sénat	senate
		(engin)	engine
		féminin	feminine
		marin	marine
		masculin	masculine
		pervers	perverse
		univers	universe
		vers	verse
		revenu	revenue
		tissu	tissue
		salut	salute
		statut	statute
		complet	complete
		concret	concrete
		futur	future
		obscur	obscure
		cours	course
		recours	recourse
		laps	lapse
		sens	sense
-	h	hourra	hurrah
		kaki	khaki
		paria	pariah
		rime	rhyme
		rythme	rhythm
-	l	assaut	assault
		bride	bridle
		participe	participle
		principe	principle
		syllabe	syllable
-	t	ancien	ancient
		tyran	tyrant

	viaduc	viaduct
various :	abcès	abscess
	abréviation	abbreviation
	abricot	apricot
	adresse	address
	anormal	abnormal
	antichambre	antechamber
	antilope	antelope
	bazar	bazaar
	cacao	cocoa
	carnaval	carnival
	cercle	circle
	ciment	cement
	drame	drama
	excentrique	eccentric
	exemple	example
	extorsion	extortion
	fontaine	fountain
	garantie	guarantee
	gouverner	govern
	hivernal	hibernal
	jauge	ga(u)ge
	langage	language
	lézard	lizard
	ligue	league
	lila	lilac
	marchandise	merchandise
	médaillon	medallion
	médecine	medicine
	monarque	monarch
	négociation	negotiation
	ornement	ornament
	parfum	perfume
	pingouin	penguin
	pique-nique	picnic
	poney	pony
	recommander	recommend
	rempart	rampart
	responsable	responsible
	restaurer	restore
	sacrement	sacrament
	transfert	transfer

APPENDIX II

DICTIONARIES

I. Monolingual

English :

scholarly : - *The Oxford English Dictionary. A New English Dictionary on Historical Principles.* 13 vols. Oxford, 1884-1928/1933 (supplements).

- *Webster's Third New International Dictionary.* Springfield, Mass., 1976.

desk : - *Chambers, Twentieth Century Dictionary.* Edinburgh, 1977.

- *Collins English Dictionary.* London - Glasgow, 1979.

- *Concise Oxford Dictionary of Current English.* Oxford, 1982.

- *Longman Dictionary of the English Language.* London-Harlow, 1984.

- *Longman New Universal Dictionary.* London - Harlow, 1982.

- *Penguin English Dictionary.* Penguin Books, 1986.

- *The Random House Dictionary of the English Language,* New York, 1983.

- *The Shorter Oxford English Dictionary,* Oxford, 1973.

- *Webster's Ninth New Collegiate Dictionary.*Springfield, Mass., 1983.

learner's : - *Chambers Universal Learner's Dictionary.* Edinburgh, 1980.

- *Longman Dictionary of Contemporary English.* London - Harlow, 1978.

- *Oxford Advanced Learner's Dictionary of Current English.* Oxford, 1989.

- *Collins Cobuild English Language Dictionary*. London - Glasgow, 1987.

French :

scholarly : - *Dictionnaire alphabétique et analogique de la langue française* (Robert), 6 vols. Paris, 1955-1964.

- *Grand Larousse de la langue française,* 7 vols. Paris, 1976-1978.

- *Trésor de la langue française. Dictionnaire de la langue du XIXe et du XXe siècle,* 15 vols. Paris, 1971 sqq.

desk : - *Dictionnaire alphabétique et analogique de la langue française.* Le Petit Robert. Paris, 1984.

- *Lexis. Dictionnaire du français contemporain.* Paris, 1984.

- *Dictionnaire de français.* Hachette, Paris, 1987.

- *Nouveau Petit Larousse Illustré.* Paris, 1985.

- *Dictionnaire du français vivant.* Bordas, Paris, 1976.

learner's : - *Dictionnaire du français contemporain.* Larousse, Paris, 1984.

- *Dictionnaire du français langue étrangère,* niveau U2. (Dubois J.). Paris, 1979.

II. Dictionaries of synonyms

English :

- CRABB G. : English Synonyms. London, 1982.
- HAYAKAWA S.I. : *Cassell's Modern Guide to Synonyms and Related Words.* London, 1968.
- HAYAKAWA S.I. : *Modern Guide to Synonyms and Related Words.* Darmstadt s.d.
- KLEIN H.W. & FRIEDERICH W. : *Englische Synonymik.* München, 1975.
- *Longman Synonym Dictionary,* London-Harlow, 1986.
- MELDAU R. : *Sinnverwandte Wörter der Englischen Sprache.* Heidelberg, 1981.

- *The Random House Thesaurus.* New York & Toronto, 1984.

- *Reader's Digest Family Word Finder.* Pleasantville, N.Y., 1975.

- *Roget's International Thesaurus.* New York, 1977.

- *Roget's Thesaurus of English Words and Phrases.* Longman, London, 1982.

- RODALE J.I. : *The Synonym Finder.* Emmaus, Pa., 1978.

- *Webster's New Dictionary of Synonyms.* Springfield, Mass., 1973.

French:

- BAILLY R. : *Dictionnaire des synonymes de la langue française.* Larousse, Paris ,1971.

- BAR E.D. : *Dictionnaire des synonymes.* Paris, 1974.

- BENAC H.: Dictionnaire des synonymes.Hachette, Paris, 1982.

- BERTAUD DU CHAZAUD H. : *Dictionnaire des synonymes.* Le Robert, Paris, 1981.

- BOUSSINOT R. : *Dictionnaire Bordas des synonymes, analogies et antonymes.* Paris, 1981.

- GENOUVRIER E., DESIRAT C., HORDE T. : *Nouveau dictionnaire des synonymes,* Larousse, Paris, 1978.

- MACE & GUINARD : *Le grand dictionnaire des synonymes.* 1984

- DE NOTER R., VUILLERMOZ P., LECUYER H. : *Dictionnaire des synonymes.* PUF, Paris, 1980.

- LAMIZET G. : *Dictionnaire des synonymes et des antonymes.* Paris, 1978.

- YOUNES G.: *Dictionnaire Marabout des synonymes.* Marabout, Verviers, 1981.

III. Bilingual Dictionaries:

- DUBOIS : *Dictionnaire moderne français-anglais, anglais-français,* Paris, 1975.

- DUBOIS-CHARLIER : *Dictionnaire de l'anglais contemporain. Anglais-français + index.* Paris, 1980.

- GIRARD : *Dictionnaire Cassell anglais-français, français-anglais,* Paris, 1978.

- *Harrap's Shorter French and English Dictionary.* London, 1982.

- *Harrap's New Standard French-English, English-French Dictionary,* 4 vols. London, 1972-1980.

- PETIT-SAVAGE : *Dictionnaire classique anglais-français, français-anglais.* Paris, 1978.

- ROBERT & COLLINS : *Dictionnaire français-anglais et anglais-français.* Glasgow, Toronto, Paris, 1987.

- URWIN : *Dictionnaire pratique français-anglais, anglais-français,* 1968.

IV. Dictionaries of "faux amis" and of anglicisms :

- BOUSCAREN C., DAVOUST A. : *Les mots anglais qu'on croit connaître,* vol.2 : *Les mots-sosies.* Hachette, Paris, 1977.

- DOPPAGNE A., LENOBLE-PINSON M. : *Le français à la sauce anglaise,* Bruxelles, 1982.

- HILL R.J. : *A Dictionary of False Friends.*London, 1982.

- HÖFLER M. : *Dictionnaire des anglicismes.*Larousse, Paris, 1982.

- KIRK-GREEN C.W.E. : *French False Friends.* Routledge & Kegan Paul, London, 1981.

- KOESSLER M. : *Les faux amis des vocabulaires anglais et américain.* Vuibert, Paris, 1975.

- LABARRE C., BOSSUYT L. : *Cut the chat, Faux amis et mots perfides,* Bruxelles, 1988.

- RANCOULE L. & PEAN F.Y. : *Les mots-piège dans la version anglaise.* Paris, 1971.

- REY-DEBOVE J., GAGNON G. : *Dictionnaire des anglicismes. Les mots anglais et américains en français.* Le Robert, Paris, 1980.

- THODY P., EVANS H. : *Faux Amis and Key Words,* London, 1985.

- THORIN A. : *Vrais et faux amis du vocabulaire anglais.* Nathan, Paris, 1985.

- VAN ROEY J., GRANGER S., SWALLOW H. : *Dictionnaire des faux amis français-anglais.* Duculot, Gembloux, 1988.

- VON WARTBURG W. : *Französisches Etymologisches Wörterbuch. Eine Darstellung des galloromanischen Sprachschatzes.* Band XVIII: Anglizismen. Basel, Zbinden, 1967.

V. Dictionary of collocations:

- BENSON M., BENSON E., ILSON R: *The BBI Dictionary. A Guide to Word Combinations in English.* John Benjamins, Amsterdam, 1986.

SELECTIVE BIBLIOGRAPHY

AISENSTADT E. : *Collocability Restrictions in Dictionaries,* in HARTMANN R.R.K. : *Dictionaries and Their Users.* Exeter Linguistic Studies, 1979, p. 71-74.

ALLEN K. : *Linguistic Meaning.* London, 1986.

BALDINGER K. : *Semantic Theory.* Oxford, 1980.

BALLWEG-SCHRAMM A. : *Aspekte einer Kontrastiven Lexicologie,* in *"Festschrift für Rupprecht Rohr zum 60-Geburtstag".* J. Groos Verlag, Heidelberg, 1979, p. 13-31.

BACQUET P. : *Le vocabulaire anglais.* Coll. "Que Sais-Je?", Presses Univ. de France, Paris, 1974.

BENSON M., BENSON E. & ILSON R. : *Lexicographic Description of English.* Studies in Language, Companion Series, 14, Amsterdam, Philadelphia, 1986.

BENVENISTE, E. : *Problèmes de Linguistique générale.* Paris, 1966.

BERLIN, B. & KAY, P. : *Basic Colour Terms.* University of California Press, Berkeley, 1969.

BERNDT, R. : *Lexical Contrastive Analysis.* BRNO Studies in English, vol. 8, 1969, p. 31-36.

BIERWISCH, M., : *Semantics,* in LYONS, J. : New Horizons in Linguistics. Penguin Books, Harmondsworth, 1970, p.166-184.

BIGGS, C. : *In a Word, Meaning,* in D. Crystal (ed.) : Linguistic Controversies : Essays in Linguistic Theory and Practice, in Honour of F.R. Palmer. London, 1982.

BLISS A.J. : *A Dictionary of Foreighn Words end Phrases in Current English.* London, 1966.

BOLINGER, D. : *The Atomization of Meaning.* Language 41.4, 1965, p. 555 sqq.

BONNEROT, J., LECOCQ, L., RUER, J., APPIA, H.& KERST, H. : *Chemins de la traduction.* Didier, Paris, 1963.

BOUSCAREN, C. & DAVOUST, A. : *Les mots anglais qu'on croit connaître,* vol. 2 : Les mots-sosies. Hachette, Paris, 1977.

BREAL, M. : *Essai de sémantique.* Hachette, Paris, 1897.

BREKLE, H. : *Sémantique.* A. Colin, Paris, 1974.

CARSTENSEN, B. : *Englische Wortschatzarbeit unter dem Gesichtspunkt der Kollokation.* Neusprachliche Mitteilungen 4, 1970, p. 193-202.

CARTER, R. : *Vocabulary. Applied Linguistic Perspectives.* London, 1987.

CATFORD, J.C. : *A Linguistic Theory of Translation : An Essay in Applied Linguistics.* Edinburgh Univ. Press, Edinburgh, 1965.

CHIROL, L. : *Les "mots français" et le mythe de la France en anglais contemporain.* Klincksieck, Paris, 1973.

CHUQUET, H. & PAILLARD, M. : *Approches linguistiques des problèmes de la traduction.* Ophrys, Paris, 1987.

CONNOR, FERRIS D. : *Understanding Semantics.* Exeter Linguistic Studies, University of Exeter, 1983.

CORNEILLE, J.P. : *La linguistique structurale, sa portée, ses limites.* Paris, 1967.

COSERIU, E. : *Einführung in die strukturelle Betrachtung des Wortschatzes.* Tübinger Beiträge zur Linguistik, 1970.

COSERIU, E. & GECKELER, H. : *Trends in Structural Semantics.* Tübingen, 1981.

COWIE, A.P. : *The Treatment of Polysemy in the Design of a Learner's Dictionary,* in HARTMANN R.K.K. : Dictionaries and Their Users, Exeter Linguistic Studies, vol. 4., 1979, p. 82-88.

COWIE, A.P. : *Polysemy and the Structure of Lexical Fields.* Nottingham Linguistic Circular, Univ. of Nottingham, 11, 2, 1982, p. 51-64.

COWIE, A.P. : *The Treatment of Collocations and Idioms in Learner's Dictionaries.* Applied Linguistics 2.3, 1981, p. 223-235.

CRUSE, D.A. : *Lexical Semantics.* Cambridge Textbooks in Linguistics, Cambridge University Press, 1986.

CRUSE, D.A. : *On Lexical Ambiguity*. Nottingham Linguistic Circular, Univ. of Nottingham, 11, 2, 1982, p. 65-80.

DAGUT, M.B. : *Incongruences in Lexical "Gridding". An Application of Constrastive Semantic Analysis To Language Teaching,* IRAL XV. 3, 1977, p. 221-227.

DARBELNET, J. : *La couleur en français et en anglais*. Journal des Traducteurs, II.2, 1957, p. 4-10.

DARBELNET, J. : *Dictionnaires bilingues et lexicologie différentielle*. Langages 19, 1970, 92-102.

DARBELNET, J. : *Lexicologie différentielle: champ et méthode*. META 18, 1-2, 1973, p. 171-178.

DEROY, L. : *L'emprunt linguistique*. Paris, 1956.

de SAUSSURE, F. : *Cours de linguistique générale*. Payot, Paris, 1968, (1ère éd. 1916).

DI PIETRO, R. : *Language Structures in Contrast*. Newbury House, Rowley, Mass, 1971.

DOPPAGNE, A. & LENOBLE-PINSON, M. : *Le français à la sauce anglaise*. Bruxelles, 1982.

DUCHACEK, O. : *Champ conceptuel de la beauté en français moderne*. Vox Romanica 18, 1959, p. 297-323.

ETIEMBLE, R. : *Parlez-vous franglais ?* Gallimard, Paris, 1964.

FILLMORE, C.J. : *Verbs of Judging : An Exercise in Semantic Description,* in Fillmore C.J. & Langendoen D.T. : Studies in Linguistic Semantics. New York, Chicago, 1971.

FISCHER, W. : *Leicht verwechselbare Wörter der englischen und französischen Sprache*. München, 1964.

FREGE, G. : *Sinn und Bedeutung*. Zeitschrift für Philosophie und Philosophische Kritik, NF 100, 25-50, 1982.

GEBHARDT, K. : *Gallizismen im Englischen, Anglizismen im Französischen: ein statistischer Vergleich*. Zeitschrift für Romanische Phililogie, 91, p. 292-309.

GECKELER, H. : *Strukturelle Semantik des Französischen*. Niemeyer, Tübingen, 1973.

GERMAIN, C. & LEBLANC, R. : *Introduction à la linguistique générale*. Montreal, 1982.

GRANGER, S & SWALLOW, H. : *False Friends : A Kaleidoscope of Translation Difficulties.* Le Langage et l'homme, 23.2.1988, p. 108-120.

GREIMAS, A.J. : *Sémantique structurale.* Larousse, Paris, 1966.

GUIRAUD, P. : *La sémantique.* Coll. "Que Sais-je ?" , Presses Univers. de France, Paris, 1979.

HADLICH, R.L. : *Lexical Contrastive Analysis.* Modern Language Journal XLIX. 7, 1965, p. 426-429.

HANKS, P. : *To what Extent Does A Dictionary Definition Define ?* in Hartmann, R.K.K. : *Dictionaries and their Users.* Exeter Linguistic Studies, vol. 4, 1979, p. 32-38.

HANSEN, B. et al.: *Englische Lexicologie. Einführung in die Wortbildung und Lexikalische Semantik.* Leipzig, 1985.

HARTMANN, R.K.K., (ed.) : *Dictionaries and their Users.* Exeter Linguistic Studies, Vol. 4, University of Exeter, 1979.

HARTMANN, R.K.K., (ed.) : *Lexicography: Principles and Practice.* Academic Press, London, New York, 1983.

HARTMANN, R.K.K. : *Style Values : Linguistic Approaches and Lexicographical Practice.* Applied Linguistics 2.3, 1981, p. 263-273.

HAUGEN, E. : *The Analysis of Linguistic Borrowing.*Language, vol. 26, 1950, p. 210-231.

HJELMSLEV, L. : *Prolegomena to a theory of language.* Madison, 1943.

HÖFLER, M. : *Dictionnaire des Anglicismes.* Larousse, Paris, 1982.

HOLEC, H. : *Structures lexicales et enseignement du vocabulaire.* Mouton, The Hague, 1974.

HUGHES, G. : *Words in Time. A Social History of the English Vocabulary.* Blackwell, Oxford, 1988.

IAROVOCI, E. & MIHAILA, R. : *Introduction to a Contrastive Analysis of the English and Romanian Vocabularies.* Analele Universitatii Bucuresti, Limbi germanice 19, 1970, p. 23-37.

IKEGAMI, Y. : *"Meaning" for the Linguist and "Meaning" for the Antropologist",* in "Language and Thought. Antropological Issues". Mouton, Den Haag, 1977.

JAIN, M.P. : *On Meaning in the Foreign Learner's Dictionary.* Applied Linguistics II. 3, 1981, p. 274-286.

JAMES, C. : *Contrastive Analysis.* Longman, London, 1980.

JOOS, M. : *The Five Clocks.* Bloomington, 1962.

KEMPSON, R.M. : *Semantic Theory.* Cambridge Univ. Press, Cambridge, 1977.

KERBRAT-ORECCHIONI : *La connotation.* Presses universitaires de Lyon, 1977.

KIPFER, B.A. : *Workbook on Lexicography.* Exeter Linguistic Studies, vol. 8, University of Exeter, 1984.

KIRK-GREEN, C.W.E. : *French False Friends.* Routledge & Kegan Paul, London, 1981.

KOESSLER, M. : *Les faux amis des vocabulaires anglais et américains.* Vuibert, Paris, 1975.

KRZESZOWSKI, T.P. : *What Do We Need Lexical Contrastive Sudies For ?* Papers and Studies in Contrastive Linguistics, Vol. 14, 1981, p. 133-148.

KRZESZOWSKI, T.P. : *Tertium Comparationis,* in Fisiak J. : Contrastive Linguistics. Prospects and Problems. Berlin, New York, Amsterdam, 1984, p. 301-313.

KÜHLWEIN, W., WILLS, W. & al. (eds.) : *Kontrastive Linguistik und Uebersetzungswissenschaft,* W. Fink, München, 1981.

LADO, R. : *Linguistics across Cultures.* The Univ. of Michigan Press, Ann Arbor, 1957.

LEDENT, R. : *Comprendre la sémantique.* Marabout, Verviers, 1974.

LEECH, G.N. : *Semantics.* Penguin Harmondsworth, 1974.

LEHRER, A. : *Semantic Fields and Lexical Structures.* North Holland, Amsterdam, London, New York, 1974.

LEISI, E. : *Der Wortinhalt. Seine Struktur im Deutschen und Englischen.* Quelle & Meyer, Heidelberg, 1971.

LEISI, E. : *Praxis der Englischen Semantik.* Heidelberg, 1973.

LYONS, J. : *Introduction to Theoretical Linguistics.* Cambridge Univ. Press, London & New York, 1968.

LYONS, J. : *Language and Linguistics*. Cambridge University Press, 1981.

LYONS, J. : *Semantics* (2 vols.). Cambridge Univ. Press, London & New York, 1977.

MACKENZIE, F. : *Les relations de l'Angleterre et de la France d'après le vocabulaire*. Droz, Paris, 1939.

MARTINET, A. : *Eléments de linguistique générale*. A. Collin, Paris, 1960.

Mc CAWLEY, J. : *Where do Noun Phrases Come from ?* in Jacobs & Rosenbaum, eds. : *Readings in English Transformational Grammar*. New York, 1970.

Mc DAVID, R.I. & DUCKERT, A.R. : *Lexicography in English*. New York, 1973.

MITCHELL, T.F. : *Linguistic "Goings On" : Collocations and Other Lexical Matters Arising on the Syntagmatic Record*. Archivum Linguisticum II, 1971, p. 35-69.

MOUNIN, G. : *Clefs pour la sémantique*. Seghers, Paris, 1972.

NIDA, E. : *Componential Analysis of Meaning*. Mouton, The Hague, 1975.

NOWAKOWSKI, M. : *The Lexicon and Contrastive Language Studies*. Papers and Studies in Contrastive Linguistics 6, 1977, p. 25-42.

OGDEN, C.K. & RICHARD, I.A. : *The Meaning of Meaning*. Kegan Paul, London, 1923.

OLSCHANSKI, I.G. : *Die Konfrontative Wortschatzanalyse und die zweisprachige Lexikographie*. Deutsch als Fremdsprache 12.6, 1975, 375-379.

PALMER, F.R. : *Semantics*. Cambridge Univ. Press, Cambridge, London, New York, 1981.

PERGNIER, M. : *Les anglicismes*. Presses Universitaires de France, Paris, 1989.

POTTIER, B. : *Recherches sur l'analyse sémantique en linguistique et en traduction mécanique*. Nancy, 1963.

QUEMADA, B. : *Lexicology and Lexicography*. in T.A. Sebeok et al., eds., *"Current Trends in Linguistics"*. vol. 9, p. 395-475 Mouton, The Hague, 1972.

RAABE, H. : *Trends in Kontrastive Linguistik I.* Tübingen, 1974.

RAFROIDI, P., PLAISANT, M. & SHORT, D.J. : *Nouveau manuel de l'angliciste.* Ophrys, Paris, 1986.

RANCOULE, L. & PEAN, F.Y. : *Les mots-pièges dans la version anglaise.* Paris, 1971.

RASMUSSEN, J. : *Essai d'une typologie des "faux-amis" danois-français.* C.E.B.A.L. 4, Copenhagen 1978, p. 7-21.

REY, A. : *La lexicologie.* Lectures, Paris, 1970.

REY-DEBOVE, J. : *La sémiotique de l'emprunt lexical.* Travaux de linguistique et de littérature, vol. 11, 1973, p. 109-123.

REY-DEBOVE, J. & GAGNON, G. : *Dictionnaire des Anglicismes.* Le Robert, Paris, 1980.

RICKEN, U. : *Französische Lexikologie.* Leipzig, 1983.

ROBINSON, R. : *Definition.* Clarendon Press. Oxford, 1962.

ROSCH, E.H., MERVIS, C.B., GRAY, W.D., JOHNSON, D.M. & BOYES-BRAEM, P. : *Basic Objects in Natural Categories.* Cognitive Psychology 8, 1976, p. 259-270.

SCHEPPING, M.T. : *Das Lexikon im Sprachvergleich,* in Schwarze C. & Wunderlich, D., "Handbuch der Lexikologie. Athenäum Verlag, Königstein/Ts, 1985, p. 184-195.

SCHWARZE, C. : *Une typologie des contrastes lexicaux,* in "Allgemeine Sprachwissenschaft, Sprachtypologie und Text linguistik", Festschrift für P. Hartmann. Tübingen, 1983, p. 199-210.

SERJEANTSON, M. : *A History of Foreign Words in English.* London, 1935.

TOURNIER, J. : *Introduction descriptive à la lexicogénétique de l'anglais contemporain.* Paris-Genève, 1985.

TRESCASES, P. : *Le franglais vingt ans après.* Guérain, Montreal, 1982.

TRIER, J. : *Der Deutsche Wortschatz im Sinnbezirk des Verstandes.* Heidelberg, 1931.

ULLMANN, S. : *Précis de sémantique française.* Berne, 1969.

ULLMANN, S. : *The Principles of semantics.* Oxford, Glasgow, 1963.

ULLMANN, S. : *Semantics: An Introduction to the Science of Meaning*. Oxford, 1962.

VAN HOOF, H. : *Traduire l'Anglais. Théorie et Pratique*. Duculot Louvain-la-Neuve, 1989.

VAN OVERBEKE, M. : *Mécanismes de l'interférence linguistique*. Madrid, 1976.

VAN ROEY, J. : *Deceptive Terminology for Deceptive Cognates,* in Van Noppen, J.P. & Debusscher (eds.) : Communiquer et Traduire - Hommage à Jean Dierickx, Bruxelles, 1985, p. 159-167.

VAN ROEY, J. : *Le traitement lexicographique des "mots-sosies" anglais-français,* in "Langues et cultures. Mélanges offerts à Willy Bal", Cahiers de l'Institut de Linguistique dc Louvain, 10. 1-3, Louvain-la Neuve, 1984, p. 287-303.

VINAY, J.P. & DARBELNET, J. : *Stylistique comparée du français et de l'anglais*. Didier, Paris, 1972.

WALDRON, R.A. : *Sense and Sense Development*. André Deutsch, London, 1967.

WANDRUSZKA, M. : *Sprachen, Vergleichbar und Unvergleichbar*. München, 1969.

WEINREICH, U. : *Languages in Contact*. Mouton, The Hague, 1953.

WELNA, J. : *Deceptive Words. A Study in the Contrastive Lexicon of Polish and English*. Papers and Studies in Contrastive Linguistics, 7, 1977, p. 73-84.

WHORF, B.J. : *Language, Thought and Reality*. Selected Writings, edited by J.B. CARROLL, Cambridge, Mass. 1956.

WIERZBICKA, A. : *Lexicography and Conceptual Analysis*. Karoma, Ann Arbor, 1985.

WIKBERG, Kay : *Methods in Contrastive Lexicology*. Applied Linguistics 4.3, 1983, p. 213-221.

WITTGENSTEIN, L. : *Philosophical Investigations*. Blackwell, Oxford, 1953.

ZAJICEK, J. : *Notions essentielles d'anglais*. Sirey, Paris, 1965.

ZGUSTA, L. : *A Manual of Lexicography*. Mouton, The Hague, 1971.

BCILL 5: *Language in Sociology*, **éd. VERDOODT A. ET KJOLSETH Rn,** 304 pp., 1976. Prix: 760,- FB.
From the 153 sociolinguistics papers presented at the 8th World Congress of Sociology, the editors selected 10 representative contributions about language and education, industrialization, ethnicity, politics, religion, and speech act theory.

BCILL 6: **HANART M.**, *Les littératures dialectales de la Belgique romane: Guide bibliographique*, 96 pp., 1976 (2e tirage, corrigé de CD 12). Prix: 340,- FB.
En ce moment où les littératures connexes suscitent un regain d'intérêt indéniable, ce livre rassemble une somme d'informations sur les productions littéraires wallonnes, mais aussi picardes et lorraines. Y sont également considérés des domaines annexes comme la linguistique dialectale et l'ethnographie.

BCILL 7: *Hethitica II*, **éd. JUCQUOIS G. et LEBRUN R.**, avec la collaboration de DEVLAMMINCK B., II-159 pp., 1977, Prix: 480,- FB.
Cinq ans après *Hethitica I* publié à la Faculté de Philosophie et Lettres de l'Université de Louvain, quelques hittitologues belges et étrangers fournissent une dizaine de contributions dans les domaines de la linguistique anatolienne et des cultures qui s'y rattachent.

BCILL 8: **JUCQUOIS G. et DEVLAMMINCK B.**, *Compléments aux dictionnaires étymologiques du grec*. Tome I: A-K, II-121 pp., 1977. Prix: 380,- FB.
Le *Dictionnaire étymologique de la langue grecque* du regretté CHANTRAINE P. est déjà devenu, avant la fin de sa parution, un classique indispensable pour les hellénistes. Il a fait l'objet de nombreux comptes rendus, dont il a semblé intéressant de regrouper l'essentiel en un volume. C'est le but que poursuivent ces *Compléments aux dictionnaires étymologiques du grec*.

BCILL 9: **DEVLAMMINCK B. et JUCQUOIS G.**, *Compléments aux dictionnaires étymologiques du gothique*. Tome I: A-F, II-123 pp., 1977. Prix: 380,- FB.
Le principal dictionnaire étymologique du gothique, celui de Feist, date dans ses dernières éditions de près de 40 ans. En attendant une refonte de l'œuvre qui incorporerait les données récentes, ces compléments donnent l'essentiel de la littérature publiée sur ce sujet.

BCILL 10: **VERDOODT A.**, *Les problèmes des groupes linguistiques en Belgique: Introduction à la bibliographie et guide pour la recherche*, 235 pp., 1977 (réédition de CD 1). Prix: 590,- FB.
Un «trend-report» de 2.000 livres et articles relatifs aux problèmes socio-linguistiques belges. L'auteur, qui a obtenu l'aide de nombreux spécialistes, a notamment dépouillé les catalogues par matière des bibliothèques universitaires, les principales revues belges et les périodiques sociologiques et linguistiques de classe internationale.

BCILL 11: **RAISON J. et POPE M.**, *Index transnuméré du linéaire A*, 333 pp., 1977. Prix: 840,- FB.
Cet ouvrage est la suite, antérieurement promise, de RAISON-POPE, Index du linéaire A, Rome 1971. A l'introduction près (et aux dessins des «mots»), il en reprend entièrement le contenu et constitue de ce fait une édition nouvelle, corrigée sur les originaux en 1974-76 et augmentée des textes récemment publiés d'Arkhanès, Knossos, La Canée, Zakro, etc., également autopsiés et rephotographiés par les auteurs.

BCILL 12: **BAL W. et GERMAIN J.,** *Guide bibliographique de linguistique romane,* VI-267 pp., 1978. Prix 685,- FB., ISBN 2-87077-097-9, 1982, ISBN 2-8017-099-1.
Conçu principalement en fonction de l'enseignement, cet ouvrage, sélectif, non exhaustif, tâche d'être à jour pour les travaux importants jusqu'à la fin de 1977. La bibliographie de linguistique romane proprement dite s'y trouve complétée par un bref aperçu de bibliographie générale et par une introduction bibliographique à la linguistique générale.

BCILL 13: **ALMEIDA I.,** *L'opérativité sémantique des récits-paraboles. Sémiotique narrative et textuelle. Herméneutique du discours religieux.* Préface de Jean LADRIÈRE, XIII-484 pp., 1978. Prix: 1.250,- FB.
Prenant comme champ d'application une analyse sémiotique fouillée des récitsparaboles de l'Évangile de Marc, ce volume débouche sur une réflexion herméneutique concernant le monde religieux de ces récits. Il se fonde sur une investigation épistémologique contrôlant les démarches suivies et situant la sémiotique au sein de la question générale du sens et de la comprehension.

BCILL 14: *Études Minoennes I: le linéaire A,* **éd. Y. DUHOUX**, 191 pp., 1978. Prix: 480,- FB.
Trois questions relatives à l'une des plus anciennes écritures d'Europe sont traitées dans ce recueil; évolution passée et état présent des recherches; analyse linguistique de la langue du linéaire A; lecture phonétique de toutes les séquences de signes éditées à ce jour.

BCILL 15: *Hethitica III*, 165 pp., 1979. prix: 490,- FB.
Ce volume rassemble quatre études consacrées à la titulature royal hittite, la femme dans la société hittite, l'onomastique lycienne et gréco-asianique, les rituels CTH 472 contre une impureté.

BCILL 16: **GODIN P.,** *Aspecten van de woordvolgorde in het Nederlands. Een syntaktische, semantische en functionele benadering*, VI + 338 pp., 1980. Prix: 1.000,- FB., ISBN 2-87077-241-6.
In dit werk wordt de stelling verdedigd dat de woordvolgorde in het Nederlands beregeld wordt door drie hoofdfaktoren, nl. de syntaxis (in de engere betekenis van dat woord), de semantiek (in de zin van distributie van de dieptekasussen in de oppervlaktestruktuur) en het zgn. functionele zinsperspektief (d.i. de distributie van de constituenten naargelang van hun graad van communicatief dynamisme).

BCILL 17: **BOHL S.,** *Ausdrucksmittel für ein Besitzverhältnis im Vedischen und griechischen,* III + 108 pp., 1980. Prix: 360,- FB., ISBN 2-87077-170-3.
This study examines the linguistic means used for expressing possession in Vedic Indian and Homeric Greek. The comparison, based on a select corpus of texts, reveals that these languages use essentially inherited devices but with differing frequency ratios, in addition Greek has developed a verb "to have", the result of a different rhythm in cultural development.

BCILL 18: **RAISON J. et POPE M.,** *Corpus transnuméré du linéaire A*, 350 pp., 1980. Prix: 1.100,- FB.
Cet ouvrage est, d'une part, la clé à l'Index transnuméré du linéaire A des mêmes auteurs, BCILL 11: de l'autre, il ajoute aux recueils d'inscriptions déjà publiés de plusieurs côtés des compléments indispensables; descriptions, transnumérations, apparat critique, localisation précise et chronologie détaillée des textes, nouveautés diverses, etc.

BCILL 19: **FRANCARD M.,** *Le parler de Tenneville. Introduction à l'étude linguistique des parlers wallo-lorrains*, 312 pp., 1981. Prix: 780,- FB., ISBN 2-87077-000-6.
Dialectologues, romanistes et linguistes tireront profit de cette étude qui leur fournit une riche documentation sur le domaine wallo-lorrain, un aperçu général de la segmentation dialectale en Wallonie, et de nouveaux matériaux pour l'étude du changement linguistique dans le domaine gallo-roman. Ce livre intéressera aussi tous ceux qui sont attachés au patrimoine culturel du Luxembourg belge en particulier, et de la Wallonie en général.

BCILL 20: **DESCAMPS A. et al.,** *Genèse et structure d'un texte du Nouveau Testament. Étude interdisciplinaire du chapitre 11 de l'Évangile de Jean*, 292 pp., 1981. Prix: 895,- FB.
Comment se pose le problème de l'intégration des multiples approches d'un texte biblique? Comment articuler les unes aux autres les perspectives développées par l'exégèse historicocritique et les approches structuralistes? C'est à ces questions que tentent de répondre les auteurs à partir de l'étude du récit de la résurrection de Lazare. Ce volume a paru simultanément dans la collection «Lectio divina» sous le n° 104, au Cerf à Paris, ISBN 2-204-01658-6.

BCILL 21: *Hethitica IV*, 155 pp., 1981. Prix: 390,- FB., ISBN 2-87077-026.
Six contributions d'E. Laroche, F. Bader, H. Gonnet, R. Lebrun et P. Crepon sur: les noms des Hittites; hitt. zinna-; un geste du roi hittite lors des affaires agraires; vœux de la reine à Istar de Lawazantiya; pauvres et démunis dans la société hittite; le thème du cerf dans l'iconographie anatolienne.

BCILL 22: **J.-J. GAZIAUX,** *L'élevage des bovidés à Jauchelette en roman pays de Brabant. Étude dialectologique et ethnographique*, XVIII + 372 pp., 1 encart, 45 illustr., 1982. Prix: 1.170,- FB., ISBN 2-87077-137-1.
Tout en proposant une étude ethnographique particulièrement fouillée des divers aspects de l'élevage des bovidés, avec une grande sensibilité au facteur humain, cet ouvrage recueille le vocabulaire wallon des paysans d'un petit village de l'est du Brabant, contrée peu explorée jusqu'à présent sur le plan dialectal.

BCILL 23: *Hethitica V*, 131 pp., 1983. Prix: 330,- FB., ISBN 2-87077-155-X.
Onze articles de H. Berman, M. Forlanini, H. Gonnet, R. Haase, E. Laroche, R. Lebrun, S. de Martino, L.M. Mascheroni, H. Nowicki, K. Shields.

BCILL 24: **L. BEHEYDT,** *Kindertaalonderzoek. Een methodologisch handboek*, 252 pp., 1983. Prix: 620,- FB., ISBN 2-87077-171-1.
Dit werk begint met een overzicht van de trends in het kindertaalonderzoek. Er wordt vooral aandacht besteed aan de methodes die gebruikt worden om de taalontwikkeling te onderzoeken en te bestuderen. Het biedt een gedetailleerd analyserooster voor het onderzoek van de receptieve en de produktieve taalwaardigheid zowel door middel van tests als door middel van bandopnamen. Zowel onderzoek van de woordenschat als onderzoek van de grammatica komen uitvoerig aan bod.

BCILL 25: **J.-P. SONNET,** *La parole consacrée. Théorie des actes de langage, linguistique de l'énonciation et parole de la foi*, VI-197 pp., 1984. Prix: 520,- FB. ISBN 2-87077-239-4.
D'où vient que la parole de la foi ait une telle force?
Ce volume tente de répondre à cette question en décrivant la «parole consacrée», en cernant la puissance spirituelle et en définissant la relation qu'elle instaure entre l'homme qui la prononce et le Dieu dont il parle.

BCILL 26: **A. MORPURGO DAVIES - Y. DUHOUX (ed.),** *Linear B: A 1984 Survey, Proceedings of the Mycenaean Colloquium of the VIIIth Congress of the International Federation of the Societies of Classical Studies (Dublin, 27 August-1st September 1984),* 310 pp., 1985. Price: 850 FB., ISBN 2-87077-289-0.
Six papers by well known Mycenaean specialists examine the results of Linear B studies more than 30 years after the decipherment of script. Writing, language, religion and economy are all considered with constant reference to the Greek evidence of the First Millennium B.C. Two additional articles introduce a discussion of archaeological data which bear on the study of Mycenaean religion.

BCILL 27: *Hethitica VI,* 204 pp., 1985. Prix: 550 FB. ISBN 2-87077-290-4.
Dix articles de J. Boley, M. Forlanini, H. Gonnet, E. Laroche, R. Lebrun, E. Neu, M. Paroussis, M. Poetto, W.R. Schmalstieg, P. Swiggers.

BCILL 28: **R. DASCOTTE,** *Trois suppléments au dictionnaire du wallon du Centre,* 359 pp., 1 encart, 1985. Prix: 950 FB. ISBN 2-87077-303-X.
Ce travail comprend 5.200 termes qui apportent un complément substantiel au *Dictionnaire du wallon du Centre* (8.100 termes). Il est le fruit de 25 ans d'enquête sur le terrain et du dépouillement de nombreux travaux dont la plupart sont inédits, tels des mémoires universitaires. Nul doute que ces *Trois suppléments au dictionnaire du wallon du Centre* intéresseront le spécialiste et l'amateur.

BCILL 29: **B. HENRY,** *Les enfants d'immigrés italiens en Belgique francophone, Seconde génération et comportement linguistique*, 360 pp., 1985. Prix: 950 FB. ISBN 2-87077-306-4.
L'ouvrage se veut un constat de la situation linguistique de la seconde génération immigrée italienne en Belgique francophone en 1976. Il est basé sur une étude statistique du comportement linguistique de 333 jeunes issus de milieux immigrés socio-économiques modestes. Des chiffres préoccupants qui parlent et qui donnent à réfléchir...

BCILL 30: **H. VAN HOOF,** *Petite histoire de la traduction en Occident*, 105 pp., 1986. Prix: 380 FB. ISBN 2-87077-343-9.
L'histoire de notre civilisation occidentale vue par la lorgnette de la traduction. De l'Antiquité à nos jours, le rôle de la traduction dans la transmission du patrimoine gréco-latin, dans la christianisation et la Réforme, dans le façonnage des langues, dans le développement des littératures, dans la diffusion des idées et du savoir. De la traduction orale des premiers temps à la traduction automatique moderne, un voyage fascinant.

BCILL 31: **G. JUCQUOIS,** *De l'egocentrisme à l'ethnocentrisme*, 421 pp., 1986. Prix: 1.100 FB. ISBN 2-87077-352-8.
La rencontre de l'Autre est au centre des préoccupations comparatistes. Elle constitue toujours un événement qui suscite une interpellation du sujet: les manières d'être, d'agir et de penser de l'Autre sont autant de questions sur nos propres attitudes.

BCILL 32: **G. JUCQUOIS,** *Analyse du langage et perception culturelle du changement,* 240 p., 1986. Prix: 640 FB. ISBN 2-87077-353-6.
La communication suppose la mise en jeu de différences dans un système perçu comme permanent. La perception du changement ets liée aux données culturelles: le concept de différentiel, issu très lentement des mathématiques, peut être appliqué aux sciences du vivant et aux sciences de l'homme.

BCILL 33-35: **L. DUBOIS,** *Recherches sur le dialecte arcadien*, 3 vol., 236, 324, 134 pp., 1986. Prix: 1.975 FB. ISBN 2-87077-370-6.
Cet ouvrage présente aux antiquisants et aux linguistes un corpus mis à jour des inscriptions arcadiennes ainsi qu'une description synchronique et historique du dialecte. Le commentaire des inscriptions est envisagé sous l'angle avant tout philologique; l'objectif de la description de ce dialecte grec est la mise en évidence de nombreux archaïsmes linguistiques.

BCILL 36: *Hethitica VII*, 267 pp., 1987. Prix: 800 FB.
Neuf articles de P. Cornil, M. Forlanini, G. Gonnet, R. Haase, G. Kellerman, R. Lebrun, K. Shields, O. Soysal, Th. Urbin Choffray.

BCILL 37: *Hethitica VIII. Acta Anatolica E. Laroche oblata*, 426 pp., 1987. Prix: 1.300 FB.
Ce volume constitue les *Actes* du Colloque anatolien de Paris (1-5 juillet 1985): articles de D. Arnaud, D. Beyer, Cl. Brixhe, A.M. et B. Dinçol, F. Echevarria, M. Forlanini, J. Freu, H. Gonnet, F. Imparati, D. Kassab, G. Kellerman, E. Laroche, R. Lebrun, C. Le Roy, A. Morpurgo Davies et J.D. Hawkins, P. Neve, D. Parayre, F. Pecchioli-Daddi, O. Pelon, M. Salvini, I. Singer, C. Watkins.

BCILL 38: **J.-J. GAZIAUX**, *Parler wallon et vie rurale au pays de Jodoigne à partir de Jauchelette*. Avant-propos de Willy Bal, 368 pp., 1987. Prix: 790 FB.
Après avoir caractérisé le parler wallon de la région de Jodoigne, l'auteur de ce livre abondamment illustré s'attache à en décrire le cadre villageois, à partir de Jauchelette. Il s'intéresse surtout à l'évolution de la population et à divers aspects de la vie quotidienne (habitat, alimentation, distractions, vie religieuse), dont il recueille le vocabulaire wallon, en alliant donc dialectologie et ethnographie.

BCILL 39: **G. SERBAT,** *Linguistique latine et Linguistique générale*, 74 pp., 1988. Prix: 280 FB. ISBN 90-6831-103-4.
Huit conférences faites dans le cadre de la Chaire Francqui, d'octobre à décembre 1987, sur: le temps; deixis et anaphore; les complétives; la relative; nominatif; génitif partitif; principes de la dérivation nominale.

BCILL 40: *Anthropo-logiques*, éd. D. Huvelle, J. Giot, R. Jongen, P. Marchal, R. Pirard (Centre interdisciplinaire de Glossologie et d'Anthropologie Clinique), 202 pp., 1988. Prix: 600 FB. ISBN 90-6831-108-5.
En un moment où l'on ne peut plus ignorer le malaise épistémologique où se trouvent les sciences de l'humain, cette série nouvelle publie des travaux situés dans une perspective anthropo-logique unifiée mais déconstruite, épistémologiquement et expérimentalement fondée. Domaines abordés dans ce premier numéro: présentation générale de l'anthropologie clinique; épistémologie; linguistique saussurienne et glossologie; méthodologie de la description de la grammaticalité langagière (syntaxe); anthropologie de la personne (l'image spéculaire).

BCILL 41: **M. FROMENT,** *Temps et dramatisations dans les récits écrits d'élèves de 5ème*, 268 pp., 1988. Prix: 850 FB.
Les récits soumis à l'étude ont été analysés selon les principes d'une linguistique qui intègre la notion de circulation discursive, telle que l'a développée M. Bakhtine.
La comparaison des textes a fait apparaître que le temps était un principe différenciateur, un révélateur du type d'histoire racontée.
La réflexion sur la temporalité a également conduit à constituer une typologie des textes intermédiaire entre la langue et la diversité des productions, en fonction de leur homogénéité.

BCILL 42: **Y.L. ARBEITMAN** (ed.), *A Linguistic Happening in Memory of Ben Schwartz. Studies in Anatolian, Italic and Other Indo-European Languages,* 598 pp., 1988. Prix: 1800,- FB.
36 articles dédiés à la mémoire de B. Schwartz traitent de questions de linguistique anatolienne, italique et indo-européenne.

BCILL 43: *Hethitica IX,* 179 pp., 1988. Prix: 540 FB. ISBN. Cinq articles de St. DE MARTINO, J.-P. GRÉLOIS, R. LEBRUN, E. NEU, A.-M. POLVANI.

BCILL 44: **M. SEGALEN** (éd.), *Anthropologie sociale et Ethnologie de la France,* 873 pp., 1989. Prix: 2.620 FB. ISBN 90-6831-157-3 (2 vol.).
Cet ouvrage rassemble les 88 communications présentées au Colloque International «Anthropologie sociale et Ethnologie de la France» organisé en 1987 pour célébrer le cinquantième anniversaire du Musée national des Arts et Traditions populaires (Paris), une des institutions fondatrices de la discipline. Ces textes montrent le dynamisme et la diversité de l'ethnologie chez soi. Ils sont organisés autour de plusieurs thèmes: le regard sur le nouvel «Autre», la diversité des cultures et des identités, la réévaluation des thèmes classiques du symbolique, de la parenté ou du politique, et le rôle de l'ethnologue dans sa société.

BCILL 45: **J.-P. COLSON,** *Krashens monitortheorie: een experimentele studie van het Nederlands als vreemde taal. La théorie du moniteur de Krashen: une étude expérimentale du néerlandais, langue étrangère,* 226 pp., 1989. Prix: 680 FB. ISBN 90-6831-148-4.
Doel van dit onderzoek is het testen van de monitortheorie van S.D. Krashen in verband met de verwerving van het Nederlands als vreemde taal. Tevens wordt uiteengezet welke plaats deze theorie inneemt in de discussie die momenteel binnen de toegepaste taalwetenschap gaande is.

BCILL 46: *Anthropo-logiques* 2 (1989), 324 pp., 1989. Prix: 970 FB. ISBN 90-6831-156-5.
Ce numéro constitue les Actes du Colloque organisé par le CIGAC du 5 au 9 octobre 1987. Les nombreuses interventions et discussions permettent de dégager la spécificité épistémologique et méthodologique de l'anthropologie clinique: approches (théorique ou clinique) de la rationalité humaine, sur le plan du signe, de l'outil, de la personne ou de la norme.

BCILL 47: *Le comparatisme*, t. 1: *Généalogie d'une méthode*, 206 pp., 1989. Prix: 750 FB. ISBN 90-6831-171-9.
Le comparatisme, en tant que méthode scientifique, n'apparaît qu'au XIXe siècle. En tant que manière d'aborder les problèmes, il est beaucoup plus ancien. Depuis les premières manifestations d'un esprit comparatiste, à l'époque des Sophistes de l'Antiquité, jusqu'aux luttes théoriques qui préparent, vers la fin du XVIIIe siècle, l'avènement d'une méthode comparative, l'histoire des mentalités permet de préciser ce qui, dans une société, favorise l'émergence contemporaine de cette méthode.

BCILL 48: *La méthode comparative dans les sciences de l'homme*, 138 pp., 1989. Prix: 560 FB. ISBN 90-6831-169-7.
La méthode comparative semble bien être spécifique aux sciences de l'homme. En huit chapitres, reprenant les textes de conférences faites à Namur en 1989, sont présentés les principaux moments d'une histoire du comparatisme, les grands traits de la méthode et quelques applications interdisciplinaires.

BCILL 49: *Problems in Decipherment*, edited by **Yves DUHOUX, Thomas G. PALAIMA and John BENNET**, 1989, 216 pp. Price: 650 BF. ISBN 90-6831-177-8.
Five scripts of the ancient Mediterranean area are presented here. Three of them are still undeciphered — "Pictographic" Cretan; Linear A; Cypro-Minoan. Two papers deal with Linear B, a successfully deciphered Bronze Age script. The last study is concerned with Etruscan.

BCILL 50: **B. JACQUINOD,** *Le double accusatif en grec d'Homère à la fin du Ve siècle avant J.-C.* (publié avec le concours du Centre National de la Recherche Scientifique), 1989, 305 pp. Prix: 900 FB. ISBN 90-6831-194-8.
Le double accusatif est une des particularités du grec ancien: c'est dans cette langue qu'il est le mieux représenté, et de beaucoup. Ce tour, loin d'être un archaïsme en voie de disparition, se développe entre Homère et l'époque classique. Les types de double accusatif sont variés et chacun conduit à approfondir un fait de linguistique générale: expression de la sphère de la personne, locution, objet interne, transitivité, causativité, etc. Un livre qui intéressera linguistes, hellénistes et comparatistes.

BCILL 51: **Michel LEJEUNE,** *Méfitis d'après les dédicaces lucaniennes de Rossano di Vaglio*, 103 pp., 1990. Prix: 400,- FB. ISBN 90-6831-204-3.
D'après l'épigraphie, récemment venue au jour, d'un sanctuaire lucanien (-IVe/ Ier s.), vues nouvelles sur la langue osque et sur le culte de la déesse Méfitis.

BCILL 52: *Hethitica* X.

BCILL 53: **Albert MANIET**, *Phonologie quantitative comparée du latin ancien*, 1990, 362 pp. Prix: 1150 FB. ISBN 90-6831-225-1.
Cet ouvrage présente une statistique comparative, accompagnée de remarques d'ordre linguistique, des éléments et des séquences phoniques figurant dans un corpus latin de 2000 lignes, de même que dans un état plus ancien de ce corpus, reconstruit sur base de la phonétique historique des langues indo-européennes.

SÉRIE PÉDAGOGIQUE DE L'INSTITUT DE LINGUISTIQUE DE LOUVAIN (SPILL).

SPILL 1: **G. JUCQUOIS,** avec la collaboration de **J. LEUSE**, *Conventions pour la présentation d'un texte scientifique*, 1978, 54 pp. (épuisé).

SPILL 2: **G. JUCQUOIS**, *Projet pour un traité de linguistique différentielle*, 1978, 67 pp. Prix: 170,- FB.
Exposé succinct destiné à de régulières mises à jour de l'ensemble des projets et des travaux en cours dans une perspective différentielle au sein de l'Institut de Linguistique de Louvain.

SPILL 3: **G. JUCQUOIS,** *Additions 1978 au «Projet pour un traité de linguistique différentielle»,* 1978, 25 pp. Prix: 70,- FB.

SPILL 4: **G. JUCQUOIS,** *Paradigmes du vieux-slave*, 1979, 33 pp. Prix: 100,- FB.
En vue de faciliter l'étude élémentaire de la grammaire du vieux-slave et de permettre aux étudiants d'en identifier rapidement les formes, ce volume regroupe l'ensemble des paradigmes de cette langue liturgique.

SPILL 5: **W. BAL - J. GERMAIN**, *Guide de linguistique*, 1979, 108 pp. Prix: 275,- FB.
Destiné à tous ceux qui désirent s'initier à la linguistique moderne, ce guide joint à un exposé des notions fondamentales et des connexions interdisciplinaires de cette science une substantielle documentation bibliographique sélective, à jour, classée systématiquement et dont la consultation est encore facilitée par un index détaillé.

SPILL 6: **G. JUCQUOIS - J. LEUSE,** *Ouvrages encyclopédiques et terminologiques en sciences humaines*, 1980, 66 pp. Prix: 165,- FB.
Brochure destinée à permettre une première orientation dans le domaine des diverses sciences de l'homme. Trois sortes de travaux y sont signalés: ouvrages de terminologie, ouvrages d'introduction, et ouvrages de type encyclopédique.

SPILL 7: **D. DONNET**, *Paradigmes et résumé de grammaire sanskrite,* 64 pp., 1980. Prix: 160,- FB.
Dans cette brochure, qui sert de support à un cours d'initiation, sont envisagés: les règles du sandhi externe et interne, les paradigmes nominaux et verbaux, les principes et les classifications de la composition nominale.

SPILL 8-9: **L. DEROY,** *Padaśas. Manuel pour commencer l'étude du sanskrit même sans maître*, 2 vol., 203 + 160 pp., 2e éd., 1984. Prix: 1.090,- FB., ISBN 2-87077-274-2.
Méthode progressive apte à donner une connaissance élémentaire et passive du sanskrit (en transcription). Chaque leçon de grammaire est illustrée par des textes simples (proverbes, maximes et contes). Le second volume contient un copieux lexique, une traduction des textes (pour contrôle) et les éléments pour étudier, éventuellement, à la fin, l'écriture nâgarî.

SPILL 10: *Langage ordinaire et philosophie chez le second WITTGENSTEIN. Séminaire de philosophie du langage 1979-1980,* **édité par J.F. MALHERBE,** 139 pp., 1980. Prix: 350,- FB. ISBN 2-87077-014-6.
Si, comme le soutenait Wittgenstein, **la signification c'est l'usage**, c'est en étudiant l'usage d'un certain nombre de termes clés de la langue du philosophe que l'on pourra, par-delà le découpage de sa pensée en aphorismes, tenter une synthèse de quelques thèmes majeurs des **investigations philosophiques.**

SPILL 11: **J.M. PIERRET,** *Phonétique du français. Notions de phonétique générale et phonétique du français,* V-245 pp. + 4 pp. hors texte, 1985. Prix: 550,- FB. ISBN 2-87077-018-9.
Ouvrage d'initiation aux principaux problèmes de la phonétique générale et de la phonétique du français. Il étudie, en outre, dans une section de phonétique historique, l'évolution des sons, du latin au français moderne.

SPILL 12: **Y. DUHOUX**, *Introduction aux dialectes grecs anciens. Problèmes et méthodes. Recueil de textes traduits,* 111 pp., 1983. Prix: 280,- FB. ISBN 2-87077-177-0.
Ce petit livre est destiné aux étudiants, professeurs de grec et lecteurs cultivés désireux de s'initier à la dialectologie grecque ancienne: description des parlers; classification dialectale; reconstitution de la préhistoire du grec. Quatorze cartes et tableaux illustrent l'exposé, qui est complété par une bibliographie succincte. La deuxième partie de l'ouvrage rassemble soixante-huit courtes inscriptions dialectales traduites et accompagnées de leur bibliographie.

SPILL 13: **G. JUCQUOIS,** *Le travail de fin d'études. Buts, méthode, présentation,* 82 pp., 1984. Prix: 230,- FB. ISBN 2-87077-224-6.
Les étudiants se posent souvent la question des buts du travail de fin d'études: quel est le rôle de ce travail dans leur formation, comment rassembler les informations nécessaires, comment les traiter, comment les présenter? Voilà quelques unes des grandes questions auxquelles on tente de répondre.

SPILL 14: **J. VAN ROEY,** *French-English Contrastive Lexicology. An Introduction,* 145 pp., 1990. Prix: 460,- FB. ISBN 90-6831-269-3
This textbook covers more than its title suggests. While it is essentially devoted to the comparative study of the French and English vocabularies, with special emphasis on the deceptiveness of alleged transformational equivalence, the first part of the book familiarizes the student with the basic problems of lexical semantics.

INDEX ET CONCORDANCES DE L'INSTITUT DE LINGUISTIQUE DE LOUVAIN (ICILL).

ICILL 1: **G. JUCQUOIS,** avec la collaboration de **B. DEVLAMMINCK et de J. LEUSE,** *La transcription des langues indo-européennes anciennes et modernes: normalisation et adaptation pour l'ordinateur.* 1980, 109 pp. Prix: 600,- FB.

ICILL 2: **E. NIEUWBORG et J. WEISSHAUPT**, avec la collaboration de **D. REULEN,** *Concordantielijst van Zuidnederlandse Romans:* **H. CLAUS,** *Natuurgetrouwer; De Zwarte Keizer; Het jaar van de Kreeft*, 1979, 12 pp. + 3.435 pp. en 14 microfiches. Prix: 1.000,- FB.

ICILL 3: **G. JUCQUOIS et B. DEVLAMMINCK,** *Die Sprache I (1949) - 20 (1974):* index des formes, 1979, xvi-301 pp. Prix: 1.000,- FB.

ICILL 4: **E. NIEUWBORG et J. WEISSHAUPT**, avec la collaboration de **D. REULEN**, Concordance de: G. CESBRON, *Notre prison et un royaume.* Concordance de *G. BERNANOS, L'imposture.* 1981, 12 pp. + 3.176 pp. en 12 microfiches. Prix: 950,- FB.

ICILL 6: **E. NIEUWBORG et J. WEISSHAUPT**, avec la collaboration de **R. REULEN**, Concordantielijsten van weekbladen en krantentaal (Zuidnederlands taalgebied). 1981, 12 pp. + 2.606 pp. en 11 microfiches. Prix: 800,- FB.

ICILL 11: **E. NIEUWBORG et J. WEISSHAUPT**, avec la collaboration de **R. REULEN**, Concordantielijsten van Zuidnederlandse letterkunde - Hubert LAMPO, *De komst van Joachim Stiller. Er is méér, Horatio.* 1981, 16 × 24, 12 pp. + 2.403 pp. en 10 microfiches. Prix: 800,- FB.

ORIENTALISTE, P.B. 41, B-3000 Leuven